DISCUSSION PAPER 48

Gender Violence and HIV/AIDS in Post-Conflict West Africa

Issues and Responses

BABATUNDE A. AHONSI

NORDISKA AFRIKAINSTITUTET, UPPSALA 2010

Indexing terms

Post-conflict reconstruction
Violence against women
Sexual abuse
Sexually transmitted diseases
Hiv
Aids
Women's health
Gender analysis
Liberia
Sierra Leone

The opinions expressed in this volume are those of the author
and do not necessarily reflect the views of Nordiska Afrikainstitutet.

Language checking: Peter Colenbrander
ISSN 1104-8417
ISBN 978-91-7106- 665-7
© the author and Nordiska Afrikainstitutet 2010
Grafisk Form Elin Olsson
Print on demand, Lightning Source UK Ltd.

Contents

Foreword

This Discussion Paper is based on an analysis of the sexual and gender dimensions of the civil wars in two West African countries, Liberia (1989-96, 1999-2003) and Sierra Leone (1997-2002). It critically examines the impact of, and linkages between conflict, the incidence of sexual violence against women (SVAW) and risks of exposure to HIV/AIDS in both countries. It also examines these connections in the context of post-conflict transitions. In this regard, it interrogates some of the assumptions about the linkages between war, levels of SVAW and the prevalence of HIV/AIDS. The critical perspective adopted in this paper opens up new vistas in the form of a gendered analysis of a largely neglected aspect of post-conflict transitions in Africa.

The paper provides an informed evaluation of the extent to which conflict and post-conflict transitions in Liberia and Sierra Leone increased or reduced SVAW, and if this transition has had any association with the prevalence of HIV/AIDS. Noting some of the challenges, the author is able to draw on existing data from both countries, UNAIDS, the World Health Organization and field-work data to show that in spite of over a decade of armed conflict, the indicators for both Liberia and Sierra Leone suggest they have some of the lowest adult HIV prevalence rates in West Africa. This is partly explained by the moderating influence of "the social ecology of the region, the bio-social context, and war-induced isolation of some rural communities that moderated the possible effects of conflict-induced factors that promote HIV transmission".

However, in spite of the relatively lower rates of HIV infection, the study does confirm that when subjected to age-differentials, HIV prevalence in both countries, to some extent, can be linked to partner violence, and "exploitative transactional sexual relations between older and rich(er) men and several much younger and poor(er) women". This finding is explored further in terms of its public health and human rights implications. It is argued that since women in abusive or exploitative, unequal sexual relationships are more likely to be infected by HIV, their rights and protection should constitute an important aspect of post-conflict transitions.

By drawing attention to the complexity of the connections between war, post-conflict transitions and SVAW, the study makes the important point that women experiencing sexual violence face a higher risk of HIV infection. Also important is the need for donors and policy-makers to integrate responses to gender-based violence into the support and decisions regarding HIV/AIDS prevention and treatment programmes, particularly in post-conflict contexts, where young and poor(er) women remain particularly vulnerable.

Cyril I. Obi, Senior Researcher
Leader of the Research Cluster on Conflict, Displacement and Transformation
The Nordic Africa Institute, Uppsala

Introduction

The protracted and largely interlinked wars in Liberia and Sierra Leone between the late 1980s and the first years of the 21st century had multiple and severely adverse consequences for human security and social well-being in both countries. Two of the most direct and health-harming impacts were sexual violence against women (SVAW) and HIV transmission, which disproportionately affected young women and girls. The two wars were particularly characterised by widespread and vicious forms of sexual violence on the part of all the warring factions and militias and created several other related conditions, such as large-scale population displacements, destabilisation of sexual norms and acute economic desperation that made both the military and civilian population more vulnerable to HIV/AIDS. Moreover, contrary to conventional wisdom, the transition from war to relative peace seemed to foster the persistence of women's exposure to chronic sexual violence, despite the cessation of mass-atrocity sexual crimes with potential implications for increased HIV transmission.

A key proposition therefore needing to be fully explored is whether post-conflict transitions are conducive to the mutually reinforcing but complex interactions between sexual violence and HIV transmission at the individual level. The possibility that these intersections may not operate with equal force at the population level implies that significant attention should be paid in post-conflict reconstruction and development programmes in Liberia and Sierra Leone to sexual violence in particular and gender inequality as a whole. This would modify the present situation in which HIV/AIDS enjoys far more programmatic and funding attention.

It is argued that without comprehensively addressing the gender aspects of human security, especially sexual violence against women and girls, it would be nearly impossible for Liberia and Sierra Leone to make a successful transition from conflict termination to sustainable peace and development. The point is emphasized that human security in the post-conflict context, particularly for women and girls, is less about the absence of open intergroup conflict and more about personal safety and freedom from violence, preventable morbidity and mortality and material deprivation.

The paper develops its central thesis by firstly defining the key concepts within a gender analysis of the consequences of war, and the transition from one phase of post-conflict to another, in relation to the conditions that may or may not elevate the risks of sexual violence and HIV/AIDS. The nature of the evidence regarding the main factors possibly implicated in the higher vulnerability of women and girls to sexual violence and HIV in Liberia and Sierra Leone during and after the wars is then examined to show the gaps and the difficulties these represent for arriving at firm conclusions and generalisations. Next, the paper examines the sexual and gender dimensions of the wars as a prelude to analysing the levels and patterns of SVAW and HIV prevalence during the *emergency and stabilisation* phase, the *transition and recovery* phase and the *peace and development* phase of post-conflict transition in both countries. It then briefly discusses some key issues in the main policy and programmatic responses by the governments, international aid agencies and local civil society organisations to SVAW, HIV and their intersections. Finally, the paper considers the implications of its main conclusions regarding approaches to understanding and managing the human security aspects of post-conflict transitions.

Key Concepts and the Framework of Analysis

The conceptual base for our gender analysis of the interlinkages between sexual violence against women and girls and HIV/AIDS in the aftermath of the wars in Liberia and Sierra Leone is derived from the notion that peace, security and reconstruction dimensions of post-conflict transitions are directed at consolidating the foundations for social justice and sustainable development (NEPAD Secretariat, 2005). Within this frame of reference, a variant of which is elaborated as the African post-conflict reconstruction policy framework (AU-PCR framework), *post-conflict transition* is defined as the complex process of overlapping and concurrent short-, medium- and long-term steps, interventions and activities to de-escalate and prevent disputes, avoid a relapse into violent conflict, rebuild the economic base and fabric of society and ensure the progressive attainment of sustainable peace (Ismail, 2008; NEPAD Secretariat, 2005).

Each post-conflict situation is defined by its unique history in relation to the remote and immediate causes of the war, the nature of its cessation and the type and scale of external and internal responses to the challenges of transiting from war to peace (Schroven, 2006; Chand and Coffman, 2008; Colletta *et al.*, 1996). Nonetheless, post-conflict transition may be usefully broken down into three broad, sometimes overlapping, phases (emergency-cum-stabilisation, transition and recovery, peace and development) and five strategic components. The latter, which according to the AU-PCR framework have to be considered simultaneously, collectively and cumulatively to yield an insightful analysis, are: (i) security (ii) political transition, governance and participation (iii) socioeconomic development (iv) human rights, justice and reconciliation, and (v) coordination, management and resource mobilisation.

Gender analysis demands that each of the phases and strategic components of post-conflict transition be examined according to the extent to which they affect and are affected by the differences between men and women within a particular context of post-conflict transition. The differentiation pay close attention to the division of labour in the private and public spheres, living conditions and needs, and access to and control over basic and strategic resources such as income, education, information, wealth and decision-making. It equally demands attention to gender-class, gender-age and gender-rural/urban residence interlinkages and differentials in specific contexts (UNDP, 2002; Nzomo, 2002).

A key aspect of the emergency-cum-stabilisation phase for post-conflict countries is disarmament, demobilisation and reintegration (DDR). But it has been widely documented that due to the gender bias that usually characterises their planning and management, such programmes only minimally benefit female ex-combatants in Africa (Nzomo, 2002; WANEP, 2008; Mazurana and Carlson, 2004; Ward and Marsh, 2006). Many factors are implicated, including the precondition for entry being the presentation of and demonstrated capacity to assemble and dismantle weapons. This works against most women and girls who bore arms, because many played multiple roles, including providing sexual and domestic services to male combatants, and would consequently not be defined as combatants by their male leaders, DDR officials and peacekeeping troops during disarmament operations. Several studies report that many female ex-combatants had their guns confiscated by male commanders during group disarmaments and only those ex-combatants recognised by them (nearly always male fighters) were registered (Schroven, 2006; Coulter et al., 2008; Holst-Roness, 2007).

Other factors working against women in DDR programmes are the strong stigma associated with being a female ex-combatant across Africa and elsewhere, and the lack of security in disarmament camps or processing centres. These often lead to most qualified female ex-combatants self-demobilising and therefore being excluded from DDR programmes and the associated monetary, re-skilling and other benefits .

Some of the ways a *gendered* adaptation of this framework may be applied to an analysis of the interconnections between the particular phases of post-conflict transition and women's exposure to sexual violence and HIV risks are presented in Table 1 (using the emergency/stabilisation phase) to help clarify the main concepts the paper seeks to address. Accordingly, the emergency-cum-stabilisation period and either of the later phases of post-conflict transition may, depending on the context, create conditions that increase women's and girls' exposure to sexual violence or HIV/AIDS. This basic notion is critically examined throughout the rest of this paper.

The *emergency-cum-stabilisation* phase focuses on the needs of the survivors of violent conflicts such as safety, water, food, sanitation, basic healthcare and shelter. It also entails the initial rehabilitation of critical infrastructures that sustain livelihoods and the re-organisation of broken political and social systems (NEPAD Secretariat, 2005; Ismail, 2008). Safety needs during this phase are principally addressed through peacekeeping, especially disarming and demobilising ex-combatants. The latter usually involves deployment, with the consent of belligerent parties, of a multilateral mission comprising police, military and civilian personnel to supervise and monitor ceasefire implementation, separation of forces and other peace agreements, including DDR. This phase typically lasts three to 12 months.

Table 1

En-*gendered* Application of African Post-Conflict Transition Framework with reference to SVAW and HIV/AIDS during the Emergency Phase

Elements of the emergency phase and possible sexual violence and HIV dimensions

Strategic component	Sexual violence	HIV/AIDS
Security	Peacekeepers fuel sex trade or a safer context helps to curtail rape	Ex-combatants return home with HIV or more stable and safer sexual relations as spouses are reunited
Political Transition, Governance and Participation	Women's under-representation in new structures leads to continued tolerance of SVAW or women's prominence in the political transition triggers push for more women-friendly security agencies and practices	Women's invisibility results in low attention to their greater vulnerability to HIV or women's active participation in constitutional review gives visibility to the cause of women living with HIV and the issue of AIDS stigma
Socioeconomic Development	Food aid deliveries discourage survival sex by young girls or healthcare needs of wartime rape survivors are ignored, further traumatising them	Focus on basic medical supplies produces inattention to blood safety issues for women requiring transfusion during birth deliveries or HIV-testing kit and condom supplies kickstart HIV prevention services
Human Rights, Justice and Reconciliation	The drive for general amnesty for all perpetrators of war crimes sustains a climate of impunity over SVAW or the push for special courts to try war criminals implicated in mass rapes produces the opposite effect	Women infected with HIV by soldiers during the war are offered compensation and rehabilitation or too much focus on political rights within reconciliation processes leads to the neglect of social rights in ways that foster HIV-related stigma
Coordination, Management and Resource mobilisation	Non-sharing of information among key stakeholders results in non-response to women's groups' call for prioritising SVAW as a cross-cutting issue or NGOs, including women's groups, are fully engaged by donors and the government in policy formulation and implementation leading to priority for SVAW as a cross- cutting issue by key stakeholders	New donor funding for HIV action leads to proliferation of small, poorly managed HIV projects with limited scale-up potential or slowly increasing internal and external funding and policy attention to HIV focused on expanding condom use and prevention of mother-to-child transmission as more funding becomes available

Source: Author's analysis based on certain recurring themes in the literature

The research literature generally portrays this immediate post-war period as involving higher risk of exposure to sexual violence for women and girls. This is usually attributed to increased refugee, internally displaced person (IDP) and ex-combatant movements, tensions over destabilised gender norms and roles, widespread unemployment and economic desperation, disrupted and destroyed social networks, widespread availability of small arms and light weapons and state incapacity to provide basic services and security (Ward, 2002; UNDP, 2002; Amnesty International, 2005; McInnes, 2009).

Often further highlighted is the increased violence against women due to the reintegration of male ex-combatants without necessary psychological services and the environment of impunity created by the non-prosecution of wartime perpetrators of organised rape and sexual violence. But, as illustrated in Table 1, their return may help to re-establish more stable and safer sexual relations as spouses are reunited and the presence of peacekeepers helps guard against mass sexual atrocities. Similarly, other strategic components of the post-conflict emergency phase , such as food aid deliveries as part of socioeconomic development, may discourage survival sex among women and girls or may shift the focus from the psychological and healthcare needs of wartime rape victims. In addition, while the drive for general amnesty for perpetrators of war crimes (as in 1996-97 Liberia) during the emergency and stabilisation phase may foster impunity over SVAW, the push for special courts to try war crimes suspects (as in post-2002 Sierra Leone) may have the opposite effect.

Regarding the presumed SVAW-HIV/AIDS interlinkages, several recent studies have raised doubts about the association between increased sexual violence during and immediately after conflict and the higher prevalence of HIV (Barnett and Prins, 2005; Garrett, 2005; Becker *et al.*, 2008; Whiteside *et al.*, 2006; Spiegel *et al.*, 2007; McInnes, 2009; and Nanjakululu, 2008) highlighted in several studies, especially prior to 2005 (Docking, 2001; Amowitz *et al.*, 2002; Elbe, 2002, 2003; Feldbaum *et al.*, 2006). Insights from the latter studies implied (as shown in Table 1) that the presence of peacekeepers fuelled sex trade-related HIV transmission and the return of ex-combatants, refugees and IDPs to their home communities heightened the general risk of HIV transmission. However, closer scrutiny of epidemiological evidence and insights from statistical modelling seem to indicate that the military do not necessarily have higher HIV prevalence than civilian populations and widespread conflict-related population displacements and rapes do not directly increase aggregate HIV prevalence (Barnett and Prins, 2005; McInnes, 2009). Instead, as the postulations in Table 1 derived from these studies indicate, the increased invisibility and vulnerability of women during the post-conflict stabilisation phase may elevate their risk of HIV infection.

As for the *transition and recovery* phase, it is mainly characterised by systematic efforts to rebuild the capacity of state agencies and non-state actors to enable them to recover from crisis and prevent relapse into chaos and system-wide service delivery failure by linking emergency and stabilisation programmes to long-term development plans and interventions. It also involves efforts to set up new governance structures and drafting a new constitution by an appointed interim government, followed by the signing of peace agreements democratic elections and the ushering in of a new civilian administration (NEPAD Secretariat, 2005). Typically, this phase lasts from one to three years, and ends with the transition from interim government to democratically elected administration. Much effort is made by stakeholders, especially donors, to recreate a functional public bureaucracy and to make existing police, military and other security agencies more accountable and representative (Ismail, 2008). In this phase, donors, multilateral agencies and other external stakeholders begin a gradual (but sometimes hurried) transfer of g responsibility to the state's agencies.

With regard to the increased exposure of women to sexual violence during this phase, the literature not infrequently depicts the violence-triggering effect of men's role identity crisis as relative peace finds them unemployed and increasingly reliant wives' earnings (WANEP, 2008; Schroven, 2006). Also periodically highlighted is the struggle to re-traditionalise society by conservative cultural and religious forces in the face of severe destabilisation of customary pre-war gender and inter-generational norms (Schroven, 2006; Jefferson, 2004)

Table 2
An En-*gendered* Application of the African Post-Conflict Transition Framework with reference to SVAW and HIV/AIDS during the Recovery Phase

Elements of the recovery phase and possible sexual violence and HIV dimensions

Strategic component	Sexual violence	HIV/AIDS
Security	Ongoing changes in security forces allow for continued impunity for SVAW or new anti-SVAW police units signal that sexual crimes will be punished	Security sector reform ignores HIV prevention among personnel, putting more of their sexual partners at risk or early action by the sector gives it a headstart in national response to HIV/AIDS
Political Transition, Governance and Participation	Women's enhanced political participation leads to new policy responses to SVAW or focus on constitutional and electoral matters diminishes the urgency of action against SVAW	Policy neglect of HIV as setting up of new governance structures is prioritised or women's groups voice concerns about the greater impact of HIV on women and girls, leading to enhanced policy responses
Socioeconomic Development	Big reconstruction projects create new opportunities for sexual abuse of young girls by older men or rising household income as more parents work, reducing child labour-related sexual violence	Increased male labour migration fuels high-risk sexual networking or setting up HIV services targeting high-risk male groups benefits female sexual partners
Human Rights, Justice and Reconciliation	New rape and inheritance laws favour SVAW-prevention or limited justice sector reform slows prosecution of SVAW perpetrators	HIV programmes' focus on clinical services leads to inattention to stigma and discrimination issues or women's rights and other human rights NGOs take advantage of ongoing legal reforms to push for rights of people living with HIV/AIDS
Coordination, Management and Resource mobilisation	Multisectoral policy engagement with SVAW triggers establishment of national programme or gaps in prevention and management of SVAW hitherto funded and managed by hurriedly withdrawing international NGOs	Increasing external funding helps strengthen national HIV response regarding gender issues or more new HIV programme funding is for biomedical services to the neglect of women's particular vulnerability to HIV infection

Source: Author's analysis based on certain recurring themes in the literature

Thus, the point is often made that strong links tend to exist between wartime sexual violence and women's subordinate status in times of transition and recovery. The links remain strong even though this phase of fluid social processes and unstable normative systems is supposed to provide opportunities for advancing gender equality and weakening the culture of violence against women. As illustrated in Table 2, the recovery phase may witness enactment of new laws on rape and inheritance rights as part of larger processes of legislative review, justice reform and democratisation that create a social and policy environment more conducive to combating SVAW. But whether and to what extent such changes produce real benefits for vulnerable women is often a function of political will and commitment of resources by policy makers and programme managers (UNFPA, 2006).

On the other hand, preoccupation by key stakeholders with economic recovery and renewing transport and communication infrastructure may take precedence. It has been suggested that such efforts, if successful, can combine with men's resumption of multiple-partner sexual habits, women's persisting lack of power in sexual relations and expanded sex trade and trafficking networks to increase transmission of HIV (Becker et al., 2008; Whiteside *et al.*, 2006).

For the *peace and development phase*, a defining feature is the initiation and implementation of wide-ranging long-term development plans by the newly elected government to promote poverty reduction, food security, national unity, gender equality and social justice (NEPAD Secretariat, 2005; Ismail, 2008). There is an increased tempo of reconstruction, reform and development programmes in several sectors, including security, governance, socio-economic infrastructure, justice, job creation, youth and women's empowerment, and health. This phase can last from four to ten years post-conflict.

During this phase, contradictory tendencies may operate to fuel or reduce SVAW. Indications are provided in Table 3 of a number of patterns regularly reported in the literature. It is noteworthy, for example, that corruption and bureaucratic delay may fairly quickly resurface within recently reformed and reconstituted police forces in post-conflict countries. While this may lead to non-prosecution of many male perpetrators of sexual violence, women's increasing presence in political leadership positions may counteract this by ensuring that tackling SVAW remains a political and policy priority, as in post-2005 Liberia (UNFPA, 2006; Obaid, 2007; FRIDE, 2007; GoL, 2006; GoSL, 2006).

The net effect of this phase on HIV prevalence and SVAW levels depends on the extent to which economic growth benefits are equitably distributed by gender, age, income group, region, and other forms of stratification. HIV-specific and violence-related vulnerability factors would be present at levels found in times of extended relative peace but characterised by inequality and social injustice (Whiteside *et al.*, 2006; Klot and DeLargy, 2007). For example, despite the re-establishment of macroeconomic stability, the rise in poverty among female-headed households may increase the vulnerability of girls and women to HIV risk-bearing sexual behaviours. Also, as suggested in Table 3, while greater preoccupation with electoral politics and political controversies may push HIV prevention down the public agenda, new laws criminalising HIV-related stigma and discrimination may protect women living with HIV from violation of their human rights. Additionally, the availability and quality of multisectoral and integrated programmes on SVAW and HIV prevention, care and support have been well-documented globally as major factors in effective responses to these health and human rights challenges (UNFPA, 2006; Piot, 2003).

Overall, each of the three broad phases of post-conflict transition may present context-specific challenges and opportunities for reducing or elevating the risk of sexual violence or HIV/AIDS for different population categories, especially women. The examples in Tables 1-3 above support this basic proposition. However, as regards SVAW, a worldwide phenomenon, the point has to be made that it is inseparable from the gender inequality that underpins social, economic and political processes in the private and public spheres in times of peace and war (UNFPA, 2006; Krug *et al.*, 2002).

Gender inequality refers to the subordination or undervaluation of the socially constructed and context-specific roles and attributes ascribed to one gender (usually female) to those as-

Table 3
An En-*gendered* Application of the African Post-Conflict Transition Framework with reference to SVAW and HIV/AIDS in the Peace and Development Phase

Elements of the peace and development phase and possible sexual violence and HIV dimensions

Strategic component	Sexual violence	HIV/AIDS
Security	Extended period of stability leads to general decline in violent crimes, including SVAW or rising corruption within security agencies ease escape from prosecution by perpetrators of sexual violence	Well-established HIV workplace programmes in security sector reduces its role as a bridge for HIV spread within general population, especially women or expansion of security services creates new sex work contexts for more poor young women
Political Transition, Governance Participation	Women's increasing presence in politics ensures that SVAW remains a public policy priority or men's continuing monopoly of governance leads to a weakening political commitment to eradicate SVAW	HIV's public policy prominence and declines as electoral politics and political controversies intensify or NGOs backed by international development agencies use expanded democratic space to expand policy advocacy on AIDS and women's rights
Socioeconomic Development	Growing income inequalities between genders induce increase in sexual trafficking by women or increasing educational attainment by girls reduces their vulnerability to SVAW	Women's higher vulnerability to HIV persists with rising poverty levels among female-headed households or rising domestic revenue of government enables expansion of national response to HIV/AIDS, including attention to women's needs and concerns
Human Rights, Justice and Reconciliation	Justice sector reform leads to more SVAW convictions of perpetrators or a relapse into judicial red-tapeism, engendering loss of faith in legal protection by women at risk of sexual violence	New laws criminalising HIV stigma and discrimination favour women living with HIV or new legal provisions and clinical services put unfair burden on poorly informed women to prevent deliberate transmission of HIV
Coordination, Management and Resource Mobilisation	Policies and plans of action to combat SVAW are not backed by requisite funding or stronger national political leadership on SVAW issues leads to better coordination of increasing local and international NGO initiatives to eradicate SVAW	Strengthening of multisectoral national response to HIV/AIDS as both local and external funding support increase or much of new funding for HIV is for biomedical interventions leading to relative neglect of economic and social vulnerability issues that particularly affect women and girls

Source: Author's analysis based on certain recurring themes in the literature

cribed to another (usually male) based on age-old beliefs about women, men, boys and girls (UNDP, 2002; Ward 2002). It is the main driver of *gender-based violence* (GBV), of which *sexual violence* is generally thought as a subset, since it disproportionately affects women and girls both in peace and war (Colombini, 2002; Ward, 2002; UNFPA, 2006). Ward (2002:9) provides a comprehensive definition of gender-based violence:

> ... an umbrella term for any harm that is perpetrated against a person's will; that has a nega-tive impact on the physical or psychological health, development, and identity of the person; and that is the result of gendered power inequities that exploit distinctions between males and females, among males, and among females. Although not exclusive to women and girls, GBV principally affects them across all cultures. Violence may be physical, psychological, economic, or sociocultural. Categories of perpetrators may include family members, com-munity members, and those acting on behalf of or in proportion to the disregard of cultural, religious, state, or intrastate institutions.

It follows that for sexual violence as a subset of GBV to be fully understood, its gendered foundations must be well-interrogated. The WHO's World Health Report of 2002 (Krug *et al.*, 2002:149) provides a working definition of the main forms of sexual violence that clearly brings out its gendered character:

> ... any sexual act, attempt to obtain a sexual act, unwanted sexual comments or advances, or acts to traffic, or otherwise directed, against a person's sexuality using coercion, by any person regardless of their relationship to the victim, in any setting, including but not limited to home and work.

The forms of sexual violence are listed in the above WHO report, and include rape within marriage or dating relationships; rape by strangers; systematic rape during armed conflict; un-wanted sexual advances or sexual harassment, including demanding sex in return for favours, sexual abuse of mentally or physically disabled people and sexual abuse of children. Also in-cluded are forced marriage or cohabitation, including the marriage of children, denial of right to use contraception or to adopt measures to protect against sexually transmitted diseases; forced abortion; violent acts against the sexual integrity of women, including female genital mutilation and obligatory inspections for virginity; and forced prostitution and trafficking in people for sexual exploitation. Thus, an inescapable inference from the widely varied forms of sexual violence and its strongly gendered character is that it has physical, psychological, social and economic dimensions and is at root structural violence.

The hugely disproportionate exposure of women and girls to the different forms of sexual violence has been highlighted in several studies of pre-war and wartime Liberia and Sierra Leone (WANEP, 2008; Johnson *et al.*, 2008; Barnes *et al.*, 2007; Amowitz *et al.*, 2002; Gov-ernment of Sierra Leone, 2006). Our interest in this paper is to tease out the extent to which post-conflict transition in both countries has elevated or reduced levels of sexual violence against women and girls and to ascertain the extentto which observed levels of SVAW are associated with HIV prevalence. This examination is motivated by the frequent postulation that several common factors often operate in conflict-affected settings to exacerbate the risk of HIV/AIDS and sexual violence against women and girls (Michels, 2007; Duvvury, 2005; CHANGE, 2002; Docking, 2001; Barnett and Prins, 2005; Becker *et al.*, 2008; Klot and DeLargy, 2007). These factors include women's low social and economic status, forced migra-tion and the interaction between HIV and sexual violence at the individual level.

Nature of the Evidence

The main challenge here is that sound, transparent, reasonably detailed and optimally verifi-able evidence is required for a rigorous analysis of the complex intersections between sexual violence, conflict, post-conflict transitions and HIV/AIDS (Barnett and Prins, 2005; Whiteside *et al.*, 2006). Unfortunately, the relevant empirical material for Liberia and Sierra Leone before and after the wars has many gaps and limitations, making the unravelling of these interlinkages and their implications across the three stages of post-conflict transition fairly difficult.

Perhaps because of the unattractiveness to donor agencies of relatively small (prewar populations of less than 5 million) and extremely poorly governed countries, prewar Liberia and Sierra Leone never received external financial support to conduct regular nationwide surveys of sexual and reproductive behaviours. These would have provided at least reasonably reliable, fairly long time-series of national and regional proxy measures for women's exposure by age to sex, sexual violence and the sexual transmission of HIV in both countries from the late 1970s onwards. Although Liberia conducted national demographic and health surveys (DHS) in 1986, 1999/2000 and 2007, the first two elicited data mostly irrelevant to the issues under consideration. Sierra Leone, on the other hand, conducted its first national DHS only in 2008 (Macro International Inc, 2009; Bureau of Statistics and IRD, 1988: MPEA and UNFPA, 2000).

In addition the wars made it impossible for these countries, unlike most of their neighbours, to mount national HIV sentinel surveillance surveys at the beginning of the growth phase of the epidemic in West Africa (1989-91). Such surveys would have enabled them to track the dynamics of their HIV epidemics over a long period. For Sierra Leone, for example, the first HIV behavioural and prevalence survey that approximated the national situation was conducted by the US Center for Disease Control in 2002, that is, post-conflict (NAS and UNAIDS, 2006), while Liberia had its first such survey in 2007, four years post-conflict (NASCP, 2008). Moreover, regarding sexual violence, the protracted wars left no room for collecting clinical data or for conducting systematic large-scale behavioural surveys.

Additionally, for the frequently highlighted phenomenon of war-related sexual violence and its possible association with increased HIV transmission, much of the frequently cited and recycled data derive from a few ethnographic studies, eye-witness accounts by survivors and humanitarian agency field staff, rapid assessment studies by international human rights NGOs and newspaper reports. One such report was apparently the source of the oft-cited observation that emergency-era Sierra Leone had an escalating HIV epidemic as a result of widespread rape committed by infected combatants and peacekeeping troops during and immediately after the war (Barnett and Prins, 2005). The ethnographic studies and rapid qualitative assessments, on the other hand, while useful for generating research hypotheses on and insights into the experiences of women survivors of war-related sexual violence, provide no really general findings because of the few cases and limited settings they cover. It was only after the wars that a few more systematic and representative nationwide studies on these issues began to be conducted and published.

The rest of this paper draws extensively on some of these studies, including a 2001 survey conducted by the Physicians for Human Rights NGO on the prevalence of war-related violence among IDPs in Sierra Leone (Amowitz *et al.*, 2002), the recent DHS surveys (Liberia, 2007 and Sierra Leone, 2008), and a 2008 West African Network for Peace-Building survey of women survivors of the 1989-2003 conflict in Liberia (WANEP, 2008). Further insights were garnered during interviews conducted between early October and mid-November 2008 with 10 leading policymakers and programme managers in both countries. The secondary data and interview responses have been largely conceptually organised and interpreted within a gendered adaptation of the post-conflict reconstruction policy framework recommended for African countries by the NEPAD Secretariat (NEPAD Secretariat, 2005).

Overall, the evidence on the issues under focus progressively improves in quantity and quality as we move from the cessation of warfare to the later stages of post-conflict transition. The analysis is therefore inevitably shaped by the retrospective accounts of survivors of the wars, with all the associated limitations of recall lapses and subjectivity issues. To compensate for this, supplementary insights were drawn from data in official government and international development agency publications.

The Sexual and Gender Dimensions of the Wars in Liberia and Sierra Leone

Even with all the above caveats, the evidence is incontrovertible that Liberia (with its two civil wars, 1989-97 and 2000-03) and Sierra Leone (with its 1991-2001 conflict) have emerged from two of the most inhumane, ferocious and cruel conflicts in the post-Cold War era (Sesay, 2007; Nilsson, 2003; UNDP, 2007; Barnes *et al.*, 2007). The infrastructural destruction, rape, mayhem, arson and torture perpetrated during these wars rank among the most extensive in post-colonial Africa. Adolescent and young adult women were particularly exposed to extreme sexual brutality at a time when a heterosexually-driven HIV pandemic was growing within the West African sub-region. Both countries also experienced economic, infrastructural and social collapse and dysfunction that have resulted in post-conflict human development indicators in employment, income, health, education, women's status and child well-being that are among the very worst in the world (UNDP, 2008).

Much has been written about the causes and chronology of events that led to the wars (see also King, 2007; WCRWC, 2004), not all of which is central to this analysis. However, it is useful to lay out the context for the post-conflict transitions in Liberia and Sierra Leone by highlighting key factors in their descent into conflict and their eventual transition to peace, with particular attention to the sexual and gender dimensions.

The extended and interlinked conflicts in these neighbouring countries had many twists and turns, including shifting allegiances by a few of the warring factions and even a break of more than two years in Liberia. Nonetheless, most scholars share the view that multiple remote and immediate causes were implicated in the eruption and escalation of these conflicts. The main debates relate to the relative significance of each of the factors and the way they combined to trigger and affect the course of the wars. What is important to emphasize is that all of the frequently highlighted factors relate fundamentally lto the persistent denial of citizenship rights to and the severe economic and political marginalisation of particular sub-groups or social groups over several decades (see also Zack-Williams, 2008; Fithen and Richards, 2005; Norberg and Obi, 2007).

These interrelated phenomena fuelled the bitter struggles around exploitation of and access to earnings from natural resources, youth alienation and associated radicalisation as a result of exclusionary governance processes and the disproportionate impact of economic decline on the youth. These factors, alongside the intense ethnicisation of elite struggles for power, collectively and cumulatively resulted in the outbreak of war. Within such broad landscapes of social injustice and economic deprivation, women and girls were bound to suffer more than men and boys during the wars as a result of the well-established predominance of patriarchal structures and ideologies in both countries (Nzomo, 2002; Barnes et al., 2007; WANEP, 2008).

Indeed, with females making up at least half of Liberia's total population of less than 3 million at the beginning of its protracted conflict and of Sierra Leone's less than 5 million by 1991, the estimates of the number of women raped and subjected to other forms of sexual brutality (sexual slavery, genital mutilation and forced pregnancies), indicate that girls' and women's bodies were simply turned into battlegrounds. The ferocity with which sexual violence against women and girls was deployed as a weapon of war by all the factions in both wars was such that virtually every household and family trapped in these countries was directly affected. Up to 250,000 women and girls were estimated to have been victims of sexual violence in Sierra Leone during the 10-year war, with many subjected to several individual and gang rapes (Amowitz *et al.*, 2002; Barnes *et al.*, 2007). Similarly, it is estimated that between 55-75 per cent of the women trapped in Liberia were sexually violated or raped, with large numbers abducted and turned into sex slaves and/or combatants or forced into survival sex (UN Secretariat, 2006; GGoL, 2008).

Even more consequential for post-conflict transition processes of reintegration of ex-combatants and IDPs, peace-building and sustainable development is the fact that most of the extreme acts of sexual violence were perpetrated in the presence of victims' family members and many perpetrators were acquaintances (WANEP, 2008; Amnesty International, 2001).

This reality further complicates attempts to respond effectively to SVAW in the post-conflict context, either on its own or in terms of its complex interactions with HIV/AIDS.

Table 4 broadly indicates the sexual and gender dimensions of the civil wars in Liberia and Sierra Leone. It shows clearly that girls' and women's human rights and security were very adversely affected and generally much more so than those of men and boys. Women and girls were the almost exclusive targets of sexual assaults in both countries and those that joined the fighting forces did so more often through abduction than volition, especially in Sierra Leone.

But when eventually it came, did the transition from war to peace in Liberia or Sierra Leone lead to a notable decline in sexual violence against women and the potentially associated higher risks of HIV infection? An attempt is made to answer this question in the next section.

Table 4
Some Indications of the Sexual and Gender Dimensions of Wars

Dimension	Liberia	Sierra Leone
Women and girls as % of combatants	20–40	15–30
% female combatants that were abducted	30–35	> 60
Women and girls as % of IDPs and refugees	50–65	50–65
Women and girls as % of rape survivors	80–90	80–95
Extent of girls' and women's entry into DDR	20–30	< 10

Note: These estimates come from a combination of official records and sample surveys and should be treated as only broadly indicative.
Sources: Mazurana and Carlson (2004), Coulter et al. (2008), WCRWC (2002; 2004), Amowitz et al. (2002), WANEP (2008), Amnesty International (2001; 2008), Government of Liberia (2006), Omanyondo (2005) and Johnson et al. (2008).

Sexual Violence and HIV/AIDS in the Post-Conflict Transition Context

While all countries have been, at some stage in their HIV histories, low-prevalence countries, the same cannot be said of their sexual violence histories, given the deeper historical roots of gender inequality and associated norms and belief systems that propel such violence. Thus, in the absence of a long time-series of national population-specific data on sexual violence, reliance has to be placed on extensive reviews of clinical records, police statistics and survey data recently collected in both countries.

The WANEP study (2008) reviewed the findings of a number of recent surveys by WHO and the UN Population Fund (UNFPA) and analysed primary data extracted from a 2008 survey it conducted on the sexual violence experiences of women survivors of the 1989-2003 conflict in five counties in Liberia. The analysis shows that while few Liberian women still experienced such vicious forms of sexual violence as sexual slavery and gang rapes four years after the war, many are still exposed to survival sex, domestic violence and sexual harassment. This is because intimate relations have become more militarised, a legacy of the normalisation or tolerance of sexual violence that developed during the long years of open warfare. Indeed, police and clinical reports show that over 60 per cent of rape victims in recent years in Liberia are girls of less than 18 years (GoL, 2006; Ministry of Health and WHO, 2005).

Another pattern also repeatedly highlighted in several studies is that (WANEP, 2008; GoL, 2006; Johnson et al., 2008), as pointed out in Liberia's Poverty Reduction Strategy Paper (GoL, 2008: 54), "during the conflict, the perpetrators of GBV were mainly members of various fighting forces; more recently the perpetrators are ex-combatants, community or family members, teachers, and husband/partners".

The same patterns are noted about women's sexual violence experiences in post-conflict Sierra Leone in the the 2006 country report the national government submitted to the UN about its efforts to implement the Convention for the Elimination of All Forms of Discrimination Against Women (CEDAW) since 2002 (GoSL, 2006). In both countries, the conse-

Table 5

Broad trends in Adult HIV Prevalence in Liberia and Sierra Leone, 1990-2007

	Pre-War/1st Year of War			Conflict Years		Post-Conflict	
	1990	1991	1996	2001	2003	2005	2007
Sierra Leone							
Low variant estimate	---	---	---	0.7	0.9	0.9	1.3
Medium variant	0.2	0.8	1.0	1.3	1.6	1.6	1.7
High variant	---	---	---	2.1	2.4	2.4	2.4
Liberia							
Low variant estimate	---	---	---	1.0	---	2.5	1.4
Medium variant	0.3	0.6	1.6	1.4	---	3.9	1.7
High variant	---	---	---	3.1	---	5.0	2.0

Sources: UNAIDS/WHO (various years), Liberia Epidemiological Fact Sheet on HIV/AIDS and STIs (Geneva: UNAIDS and WHO); UNAIDS/WHO (various years), Sierra Leone Epidemiological Fact Sheet on HIV/AIDS and STIs (Geneva: UNAIDS and WHO).

quences for the physical and mental health and social well-being of the affected women have been adverse. These include suicidal ideation, post-traumatic stress disorder, severe gynaeco-logical problems, sexually transmitted infections, frequent nightmares, unwanted pregnan-cies, sexual dysfunction, divorce/partner abandonment, stigmatisation by the community and families and loss of self-esteem and self-efficacy (WANEP, 2008; Arowitz et al., 2002).

The context for and vicious spiral of devastation that sexual violence causes women in the post-conflict transition in West Africa is aptly captured by this concluding remark in the WANEP study of the Liberian situation:

> In the post-conflict environment incidences of sexual violence have continued to be observed. This may take the form of coerced prostitution as well as trafficking ... Women and girls who have experienced sexual violence during conflict are probably the most vulnerable of all to further exploitation ... Rape victims may be rejected by their families and communities for having "lost value". Raped women may be abandoned by husbands who fear contracting HIV, or who simply cannot tolerate the shadow of "dishonour" they believe raped wives have cast across them. With no prospects for the future, some women and girls are driven into prostitution. Victims of previous acts of sexual violence may be dulled to the dangers of entering the sex trade and hence a lowered threshold for taking this decision. (WANEP, 2008:163)

In other words, the strategic rape of women and other forms of sexual assault as weapons of war in Liberia and Sierra Leone have had adverse social, psychological and physical health consequences that continue much further into the future. Other documented aspects of the vicious cycle of sexual violence in Liberia and Sierra Leone relate to the situation women refu-gees and ex-combatants face when they return to their home villages (Nzomo, 2002; Ward and Marsh 2006). Women-returnees often have to deal with sexual, physical and emotional abuse from their husbands or partners associated with the men's abuse of alcohol out of frus-tration and a sense of insecurity resulting from being unemployed or the delayed emotional distress from war experiences (see also Johnson et al., 2008).

On the other hand, data presented in Table 5 seek to capture the underlying trends in HIV prevalence in Liberia and Sierra Leone1 since the early 1990s, when most West African countries were at their observed lowest points or baselines in the HIV epidemic, posting

---

1. Notable differences exist in the estimates of national and sub-population adult prevalence rates in Liberia and Sierra Leone for the prewar, war and postwar years (Henry, 2005; http://wwwglobalfund.org/programs/portfolio/?countryID=LBR&lang=en and http://wwwglobalfund.org/programs/portfolio/?countryID=SLE&lang=en - accessed on 3 February 2009). The WHO/UNAIDS estimates are best viewed as 'consensus' estimates and were greatly influenced by data from recently conducted popu-lation-based HIV prevalence surveys.

Table 6

Population-based Estimates of HIV Prevalence among persons aged 15-49 years by Sex

Country/Survey Year	Male	Female	All
Liberia (2007)	1.2	1.9	1.6
Sierra Leone (2008)	1.2	1.7	1.5
Côte d'Ivoire (2005)	2.9	6.4	4.7
Guinea (2005)0.9	1.9	1.5	
Burkina Faso (2003)	1.9	1.8	1.8
Ghana (2003)	1.5	2.7	2.2
Nigeria (2007)	3.2	4.0	3.6

Sources: Statistics Sierra Leone and Macro International Inc (2008) Sierra Leone Demographic and Health Survey 2008, Preliminary Report (Freetown and Calverton, MD: SSL and Macro International); Liberia Institute of Statistics and Geo-Information Services and Macro International Inc (2008) Liberia Demographic and Health Survey 2007 (Monrovia and Calverton, MD: LISGIS and Macro International); Ghana Statistical Service and ORS Macro Inc. (2004) Ghana: Demographic and Health Survey, 2003 (Accra: GSS and Calverton, MD: ORC Macro); Federal Ministry of Health, Nigeria (2008) 2007 National HIV/AIDS and Reproductive Health Survey (Abuja: FMH); Ministere de la Lutre contre le Sida and ORC Macro (2006) Côte d'Ivoire: Enquete sur les Indicators du Sida 200 (Abidjan: MLS and Calverton, MD: ORC Macro Inc.); Institut National de la Statistique et de la Demographie and ORC Macro Inc (2004) Burkina Faso: Demographic and Health Survey 2003 (Ouagadougou: INSD and Calverton, MD: ORC Macro); and Direction Nationale de la Statistique and ORC Macro Inc (2006) Guinea: Demographic and Health Survey, 2005 (Conakry: DNS and Calverton, MD: ORC Macro).

adult prevalence figures of less than 2% in the cases of Senegal and Nigeria (UNAIDS, 2001; NACA, 2008).

The adult HIV prevalence trends for Liberia and Sierra Leone estimated by WHO and UNAIDS on the basis of blood samples from antenatal clinic (ANC) attendees between the early 1990s and 2005 and population-based estimates from national demographic and health surveys in 2007 and 2008 are presented in Table 5. They show a slow but steady rise in HIV infection rates with few notable spikes (for Liberia) during the years of armed conflict followed by a levelling off in the post-conflict period for both countries.

However, a closer review of more recently elicited data reveal no definitive patterns, making it difficult to draw firm conclusions about HIV prevalence trends in both countries. For example, Liberia's 2007 ANC sentinel survey of 5,692 samples from two rural and 13 urban sites yielded a total prevalence of 5.4 per cent, while the 2007 Liberia Demographic and Health Survey preliminary report indicates a general population-based estimate of 1.5 per cent (NAS, 2008). For Sierra Leone, an ANC sentinel sero-prevalence survey in 2002 gave a figure of 0.9 per cent, while surveys conducted in 2004 and 2005 yielded 2.9 per cent and 2.5 per cent respectively (NAS and UNAIDS, 2006). Perhaps the one pattern that may be very cautiously deduced from all the available estimates is that adult HIV prevalence in post-conflict Liberia and Sierra Leone may be levelling off after an initial slow but steady increase in the first few years of post-conflict transition.

What is noteworthy about the estimates derived from recent national population-based, household surveys presented in Table 6 is that despite Liberia's and Sierra Leone's experience of over a decade of armed conflict, the adult HIV prevalence rates for both countries are among the lowest in West Africa. In fact, only Guinea has a prevalence level as low as that observed for post-conflict Liberia and Sierra Leone. Moreover, both countries have much lower prevalence rates than Ghana and Nigeria, two countries unaffected by protracted armed conflicts since the beginning of the AIDS pandemic in the early 1980s. It seems safe to say that a significant HIV transmission effect is difficult to identify or attribute to the social destabilisation and widespread sexual violence that characterised the war years in Liberia and Sierra Leone.

That over a decade of war in both countries was not associated with significant increases in HIV prevalence at the population level suggest that the larger social ecology of West Africa may have been a key moderating influence. It seems that a biosocial context characterised by relatively low pre-war HIV prevalence, the pervasiveness of the largely HIV risk-reducing

Table 7

Age-sex differentials in HIV Prevalence in Post-Conflict Liberia and Sierra Leone

	Liberia 2007		Sierra Leone 2008	
Age group	Male	Female	Male	Female
15-19	0.4	1.3	0.0	1.3
20-24	0.7	2.0	1.5	1.3
15-49	1.2	1.9	1.2	1.7

Source: Statistics Sierra Leone and Macro International Inc (2008) Sierra Leone Demographic and Health Survey 2008 Preliminary Report (Freetown and Calverton, MD: SSL and Macro International); and Liberia Institute of Statistics and Geo-Information Services and Macro International Inc (2008) Liberia Demographic and Health Survey 2007 (Monrovia and Calverton, MD: LISGIS and Macro International).

Table 8

Relative HIV risks for Liberian women aged 15-24 by recent behaviours

Behaviour	Relative risk of HIV
2 or more sexual partners last 12 months (vs. 0-1)	1.88
1st sex with man 10+ years older (vs. < 10 years)	1.42
2 or more casual sexual partners last 12 months (vs. none)	1.83
Slept away from home 5 or more times last 12 months (vs. none)	2.76
Had STI/STI symptoms last 12 months (vs. none)	1.73

Source: As for Table 7

practice of male circumcision,[2] and war-induced isolation of many rural communities may have more than offset the elevating effects (if any) of presumed conflict-induced catalysts for HIV transmission. Often noted among the latter are mass population movements, erosion of sexual norms, widespread rape and sexual violence, peacekeepers' and warring combatants' high-risk sexual behaviours, low condom use and absence of HIV services (McInnes, 2009; Whiteside *et al.,* 2006).

This general pattern of the HIV-reducing features of conflict-impacted contexts having a greater effect than their HIV-transmission features is not unique to post-conflict Liberia and Sierra Leone. There is, in fact, an increasing body of evidence for it in recent studies of several conflict-affected countries in other African sub-regions, including Angola, Rwanda and the Democratic Republic of Congo (McInnes, 2009; Becker *et al.,* 2008).

Nonetheless, it would be extremely risky to directly relate the observed trends in adult HIV prevalence in Liberia and Sierra Leone to the available evidence on levels of sexual violence against women in both countries, since the data sets that generated them generally relate to different observation periods and, in some cases, different populations. In any case, a recent comparative analysis that includes estimates for Sierra Leone shows that even with very high rates of sexual assault on females aged 5-49 years and a higher-than-average rate of HIV transmission during such acts, the HIV level in the general population would not increase by more than half a percentage point (Anema *et al.,* 2008).

---

2. Liberia and Sierra Leone belong to the cultural belt of Africa comprising ethnic groups that traditionally circumcise males and a high direct correlation has long been reported by demographers and epidemiologists as existing between lack of circumcision in men and general HIV infection levels (Caldwell and Caldwell, 1993). Several clinical investigations and multiple observational studies have shown since 2006 that male circumcision provides protective benefit of over 50 per cent against HIV infection in men (Sawires *et al.,* 2007). Caldwell and Caldwell (1993) suggested, as seems to be supported by the data in Table 6, that Côte d'Ivoire (and areas bordering it in Ghana and Burkina Faso), where universal male circumcision is not practised have HIV prevalence levels notably higher than the West African average.

This conclusion does not, however, imply that women in post-conflict West Africa are not at higher risk of HIV infection than men. Nor does it mean that intimate partner violence and sexual exploitation of younger women by older, richer men are not implicated in women's higher vulnerability to HIV. The latter pattern has been widely documented in many other countries in Africa and the wider developing world (Fonck *et al.*, 2005; Sejeebhoy and Bold, 2003).

In fact, the age-sex differentials in HIV prevalence in Liberia and Sierra Leone depicted in Table 7 point clearly to exploitative cross-generational sex as a factor in young women's higher HIV prevalence relative to young men. If this factor is allowed to gather momentum, it could later induce much higher overall HIV prevalence, given the long-wave character of the epidemic and the emerging evidence of the HIV-spreading effects of economic recovery and infrastructural development projects typical of the later stages of post-conflict transition (Whiteside *et al.*, 2006; UNAIDS, 2007). This possibility that should not be dismissed lightly in view of the recent experience of Uganda, Nigeria and populations of men who have sex with men in the United States, which suggest that declines in HIV prevalence and incidence can stall and be reversed if actions against key transmission drivers are weakened or discontinued (UNAIDS, 2006; 2007; NACA, 2008).

The data in Table 8 provide further evidence of the much higher vulnerability of women aged 15-24 to HIV infection in post-conflict Liberia and Sierra Leone based on their reported sexual behaviours in the 12 months preceding the survey and their observed HIV sero-positive status. They convey patterns unlikely to be separable from risk-bearing exploitative sexual transactions between older and usually better-resourced men and several much younger (and usually poorer) women.

It is striking that young adult women who made their sexual debut with men 10 or more years older have an HIV prevalence level 42 per cent higher than their peers, whose first sexual intercourse was with men less than 10 years older Even more striking is the hugely elevated risk of HIV infection among young women who currently sleep out frequently and among those who currently have casual concurrent multiple sexual relationships with two or more men. The sexual violence implied by these figures reinforces the point that it is gender-based, being driven by women's and girls' economic and social subordination to men. This has serious public health and human rights implications, given that evidence from across Africa indicates that women in abusive and/or fundamentally unequal sexual relationships are at least twice as likely to be HIV-positive. Moreover, when such women are known to be HIV-positive, their likelihood of experiencing violence within the family, abandonment by their spouses and social isolation tends to be significantly increased (Duvvury, 2005; PHR, 2007).

Issues in the Responses to HIV/AIDS and Sexual Violence against Women

A key question arising from the foregoing analysis is the extent to which governments, international development agencies and civil society organisations, as principal stakeholders, have seriously reflected the issue of sexual violence against women and girls and its intersections with HIV/AIDS in their efforts to reconstruct, develop and restore peace and stability to both countries. An answer was sought by analysing the responses of ten strategic informants to in-depth interviews in Monrovia and Freetown during October/November 2008.3 In addition, relevant policy documents, strategy papers, meeting reports, programme assessments, and plans of actions, produced by the two national governments and major development assistance agencies active in both countries for several years were closely examined. These sources revealed unmistakeable patterns in the dominant responses to the interconnected problems of sexual violence and HIV/AIDS in post-conflict Liberia and Sierra Leone.

---

3. Key staff of government agencies (including a deputy minister in charge of gender issues), international NGOs, donor agencies and local civil society organisations in the gender and HIV/AIDS fields were interviewed (seven in Liberia and three in Sierra Leone) using a seven-part, largely unstructured interview guide about efforts to address SVAW and HIV/AIDS and the role of various stakeholders in these during the three phases of post-conflict transition. It proved much more difficult to interview key government and local NGO officials in Sierra Leone, many of whom demanded an official letter of introduction or clearance from the 'authorities'.

For a start, both countries have since the second year of their post-conflict transitions developed multisectoral and comprehensive national policies and organisational-cum-implementation frameworks to respond to the challenges that HIV/AIDS and SVAW pose to their economic growth and social development. In fact, in both countries' current poverty reduction strategy papers these issues are clearly identified and treated as cross-cutting all the goals and strategies for achieving economic growth and social transformation (GoL, 2008; GoSL, 2008).

Regarding HIV/AIDS specifically, each country has adopted global best practices in designing a national response that goes beyond the health sector to include educational, economic, legal and socio-political action. Planning and implementation of the responses also involve people with HIV/AIDS, religious leaders, trade unions and employers, traditional rulers, youth groups, women's associations and the media. Moreover, comprehensiveness has been sought by simultaneously addressing HIV prevention, treatment, care and support, including HIV-related stigma and discrimination.

Starting in 2003, Sierra Leone, for example, with World Bank funding and technical support, instituted a national HIV strategic framework and a multisectoral AIDS commission to drive its implementation (GoSL, 2004). It drew on $15 million funding from the World Bank's Multi-country HIV/AIDS Programme for Africa (MAP) to mount interrelated interventions over 2002-06 to reduce HIV prevalence and mitigate HIV impact on persons and households infected with or affected by HIV/AIDS. In doing so, it placed much emphasis on such vulnerable groups as AIDS orphans, sex workers, the military and ex-combatants, IDPs and refugees. Of the total budget, $2 million was allocated to building government capacity to develop an institutional response, $2.5 million to line ministries for specific sectoral actions against HIV/AIDS, $4 million for HIV-related medical supplies, especially antiretroviral drugs, and $7.5 million for civil society initiatives to prevent further spread and mitigate the impact of HIV at community level.

With regard to the prevention and management of SVAW on the other hand, Liberia's national plan of action illustrates the comprehensiveness and multisectorality of policy responses adopted since both countries moved beyond the emergency and stabilisation phase of post-conflict transition (GoL, 2006). It seeks to reduce gender-based violence by 30 per cent by 2012 by instituting outreach services for psychological support and healthcare for survivors, and fostering a more responsive justice system. As a result, several ministries, including the Ministry of Gender and Development, have elaborated period-specific implementation plans and have SVAW focal points (GoL, 2008). Other relevant institutions, like the police and the judiciary, have also been fully incorporated into the national action plan.

Moreover, laws and procedures have been changed to facilitate prosecution of SVAW perpetrators. The new rape law passed in 2005 makes rape non-bailable, imposes a prison sentence of 30 years to life, and expands the definition of rape to include unsolicited intrusion of any object into a woman's genitalia. The plan also outlines strategies for treating SVAW survivors and the economic and social empowerment of women and girls to reduce their vulnerability and susceptibility to SVAW.

However, closer examination of the budgetary allocations and follow-up actions shows that implementation of the policy initiatives has been mainly at the national level for both issues, especially SVAW, with poor integration of both issues and gross underfunding of the response to SVAW relative to that for HIV/AIDS. Policy implementation has generally lagged behind targets. It has also not fully responded to the resilience of age-old women-oppressive customs and the economic realities of life for poor women and other vulnerable groups, despite the increased activism of women's groups, persons living with HIV/AIDS and human rights NGOs (Bekoe and Paragon, 2007; Ministry of Health and WHO-Liberia, 2005). The excerpts below from our interview with a gender specialist from a UN agency in Freetown in November 2008 give some sense of the gaps in the policy responses to HIV and SVAW:

> *Government is doing a lot on HIV treatment and that is where the response stops unfortunately. Thought is not given to how people are going to feed and so many women are still*

engaging in sex work just to get money to feed. There was a young girl who was raped by her uncle and her mother was persuaded by the community to cover it up since the man claimed it was a mistake and agreed to provide some money to her. It was only when the girl started becoming frequently ill that the community knew she had also contracted HIV from the rape incident. Her mother who is widowed is so poor. The girl is taking free HIV drugs but cannot go to school as she is frequently sick and ashamed.

The policies are good, but who will implement them? Government cannot do it alone and international NGOs don't understand the local customs and beliefs of the communities as fully as the local NGOs who can get to places which the former find difficult to go to. Government should not think they know it all and that Sierra Leone NGOs don't any have capacity. They should help them access resources to implement community-based programmes.

Table 9

Funding (in millions of US$) for HIV and SVAW Programmes in Liberia and Sierra Leone

Period/Country	HIV/AIDS	SGBV	Remarks
Liberia			
2007-12	---	$15.23	Amount budgeted for theNational GBV plan of action
2002-04	$7.43	---	Amount disbursed from the Global Fund Round 2 grant
2007-09	$12.1	---	As above
Sierra Leone			
2002-03	---	$2.48	Total amount committed to child protection, social welfare and gender-related programmes
2002-06	$15.1	---	World Bank funding for National AIDS Programme
2005-10	$11.71	---	Amount disbursed from the Global Fund Round 4 grant
2008-10	$3.86	---	Amount disbursed by February 2009 from the Global Fund Round 6 grant

Sources: Government of Liberia, 2006; Government of Sierra Leone, 2004; and www.globalfund.org

The highly skewed policy and funding attention to HIV/AIDS relative to SGBV (Sexual and Gender-Based Violence) is vividly illustrated in Table 9.

This disproportionate availability of funds for HIV/AIDS programmes in Liberia and Sierra Leone is largely the result of both countries, like several other African countries, being at the receiving end of one or two of the three huge international funding streams for HIV/AIDS programmes instituted from 2002 largely as a result of international AIDS advocacy (Oomman *et al.*, 2008). These are the Global Fund to Fight AIDS, Tuberculosis and Malaria (the Global Fund), the US President's Emergency Plan for AIDS Relief (PEPFAR) and the World Bank's MAP. In the case of Liberia, the Global Fund remains the primary funding source for its HIV/AIDS programmes and services, while Sierra Leone is now in a similar situation, since its funding under MAP ended in 2006. Thus far, these funding streams have tended to support HIV programmes in ways that do not adequately address gender issues, especially SVAW and its intersections with HIV/AIDS (Action Aid International, 2007).

This point is supported by our observation that by May 2004, Sierra Leone's MAP-supported HIV/AIDS programme for 2002-06 had disbursed $3.6 million to 178 civil society-led community-based projects, of which only seven explicitly addressed SVAW and women's empowerment or vulnerability reduction (GoSL, 2004). Even the country's first post-conflict national economic recovery programme, with a budget of $115.8 million over 2002-03, provided only $2.48 million (2.14 per cent) to 11 social welfare and gender-related issues, including SVAW (see Table 9).

Similarly, by 3 February 2009, of the 16 specific objectives of the Global Fund Round 6 grant to Liberia to support its HIV/AIDS response, none focused exclusively on gender or SVAW issues, despite the funding proposal's explicit acknowledgement of the higher (by 30 per cent) HIV prevalence among women in Liberia. It is therefore clear that in both countries SVAW is grossly underfunded from both national and international sources.

Put differently, the hugely increased HIV/AIDS programme funding has only minimally covered SVAW and women's disempowerment as key drivers of HIV transmission and thus afforded limited opportunity for addressing the intersection of SVAW and HIV/AIDS. The emphasis in the HIV prevention programmes in both countries is on condom use among high-risk groups such as sex workers, the military and migrant workers, abstinence or delayed sexual debut among young people and mutual fidelity among the married population. Given the exploitative nature of sexual relationships into which very young women are coerced or goaded by older, richer men in Liberia and Sierra Leone, the high incidence of rape, and the low level of condom use even in high-risk sexual relations (SSL and Macro International, 2008; LISGIS and Macro International, 2008), such approaches are irrelevant to the sexual health and safety needs of many women. Even the focus on women in the large treatment component of the Global Fund grants to Liberia and Sierra Leone is slanted more towards preventing mother-to-child HIV transmission than to enhancing the well-being of women.

Equally clearly, in these countries, which have effectively been placed under international receivership (Sesay, 2007; Ismail, 2008), post-conflict policies on HIV/AIDS and SVAW and the few follow-up programmes and services have been mainly shaped and fielded by international NGOs and UN agencies As the director of a local NGO in Liberia noted in our November 2008 interview :

> *The donors and international NGOs decide which areas and issues they prefer to work on and their decisions are binding since they control the resources. Although the Ministry of Gender is beginning to engage with these agencies around putting more of their efforts and money in areas of most need, the response has not been encouraging, even with their active membership of the inter-agency forum on GBV. Hence, they continue to focus too much on awareness creation and safe houses fo rape survivors. But we need to go beyond these to address the root causes.*

Indeed, in 2008 (that is, seven years post-conflict) membership of Sierra Leone's National Gender-Based Violence Action Committee, the multi-stakeholder body led by the Ministry of Health and Sanitation and responsible for formulating and monitoring policy on SVAW, was dominated by international NGOs. Only two local NGOs and two government agencies were represented on the 12-person sub-committee charged with drafting the national action plan on SVAW compared to eight UN agencies and international NGOs (NGBVC, 2008). In 2006, international NGOs and UN agencies also dominated Liberia's 46-person National Gender-Based Violence Task Force, with only 20 local NGOs and government agencies being represented (GoL, 2006).

In addition to the issue of local ownership of the programmes and interventions to combat SVAW and HIV/AIDS, a more serious consequence of the above situation is sustainability. The hurried withdrawal of the UN and international NGOs from both countries within three years of their general elections threatens the continued operation of the few available good SVAW services and interventions. This is especially so since most of the programmes were established in the context of emergencies and no significant efforts have been made to build local capacity to manage and expand them. This point was made in November 2008 in an interview in Monrovia with a staff member of a UN agency:

> *Most of the funding for these projects is on a sort of short-term rolling basis, which makes it difficult to involve the communities in a systematic fashion. They just go into communities and ask people to organize themselves without having involved them in the design of the planned interventions. In short, many of these programmes are taken to the communities*

or to victims of sexual violence by international NGOs who just implement them and leave without follow-up measures.

Finally, all of our informants observed that the few integrated, multisectoral programmes to combat SVAW and deal with its intersections with HIV/AIDS are small-scale and largely based in the capital cities. Also, they minimally address the key issue of the unwholesome masculinity that is widely acknowledged to be a major factor in sexual violence and women's vulnerability to HIV in post-conflict Liberia and Sierra Leone. Most respondents indicated that the more remote, inaccessible rural communities with high levels of SVAW and HIV have yet to be covered by existing programmes and services and that few of these deliberately target men with communications interventions to change behaviours.

Implications for Further Research and Policy

The foregoing analysis raises several questions that need to be explored through further research. One need is for more systematic investigation to pinpoint the circumstances or conditions under which post-conflict transitions might increase exposure of women and girls to sexual violence as well as higher HIV infection in an overall context of plateauing or declining HIV prevalence among women. What particular factors of susceptibility and vulnerability assume greater potency in specific post-conflict transition contexts by predisposing women to greater exposure to sexual violence and HIV/AIDS? Two factors of susceptibility that could be usefully considered are scale and variety of post-conflict population movements and post-conflict transition-related changes in income and educational inequalities between men and women. Key vulnerability factors may include frequency of rape, age patterns in sexual contacts between men and women, rate of transactional or survival sex by women, multiplicity of sexual partnerships among men and women, accessibility to and use of condoms and strength of HIV prevention and impact mitigation programmes.

Another gap in knowledge which, if filled, could have significant policy value, applies to the relationship between exposure to sexual assault and other forms of sexual violence during wars and women's experience of sexual violence and the associated elevated risk of HIV infection during the post-conflict transition period. Given the concentrated nature of the HIV epidemic in Liberia and Sierra Leone and much of the rest of West Africa (Wilson, 2006; Bertozzi *et al.,* 2008), and the vicious cycle of SVAW (WANEP, 2008), it would be useful to generate empirical material to establish the proportion of HIV-positive women that have suffered a continuation of sexual violence from the war years to the post-conflict transition period.

Such efforts would require specific provisions for collecting data on these issues using existing methods as well as by adopting methodological innovation and sophistication to circumvent the difficulty of eliciting reliable information on rape and other sexual violence (McInnes, 2009; Colombini, 2002). If successful, such research could yield insights very useful for designing HIV and sexual violence prevention and impact mitigation programmes better targeted at the most-at-risk groups. Unfortunately, a dearth of financial support by major donor agencies for this kind of research and related interventions remains a major challenge (Action Aid International, 2007).

Finally, it is striking that despite strong official rhetoric, robust national policies and integrated strategic implementation plans to combat SVAW and women's higher vulnerability to HIV/AIDS in Liberia and Sierra Leone, there is no commensurate commitment to funding programmes and services that actually meet the needs of the majority of affected or at-risk women. It is easy to attribute this gap to gender bias or gender blindness among mainly male policy makers and political leaders as well as to the strength and depth of longstanding patriarchal structures and norms. As made clear, however, by some of the strategic interviewees for this study, the widespread lack of capacity in gender analysis, gender planning and women's empowerment programme-development in both countries is a major factor in this unsatisfactory situation.

Regarding the policy implications of the main points in this discussion, a key issue is what needs to be done to effectively combat SVAW and HIV/AIDS in post-conflict settings, given the structural and gendered nature of some of their key drivers. As expressed succinctly in the extract below from a recent study in Southern Africa (PHR, 2007: 1), success in controlling SVAW and HIV spread and mitigating their impact is limited without systematic and sustained efforts to empower women and change men's attitudes and behaviours towards women:

> *The continuing extraordinary prevalence of HIV... particularly among women demonstrates that campaigns, scaled-up HIV testing ... and antiretroviral [ARV] treatment are not enough. Women must be empowered with legal rights, sufficient food and economic opportunities to gain agency of their own lives. Men must be educated and supported to acknowledge women's equal status and throw off the yoke of socially- and culturally-sanctioned discriminatory beliefs and risky sexual behaviour.*

In other words, programmes to combat HIV/AIDS and SVAW need to go beyond individual behaviours by addressing social and economic vulnerabilities, mobilising communities and new partnerships and providing additional opportunities, resources and services to address the specific needs of women and girls. Such efforts must be systematically integrated to be effective and sustainable, given the mutually reinforcing relationship between SVAW and HIV/AIDS. In particular, integrating the strategies to reduce SVAW into ongoing and planned HIV prevention and treatment programmes in post-conflict Liberia and Sierra Leone is likely to enable these health interventions to achieve their full potential and at the same time tackle a broader human rights and public health issue.

The emphasis in the Global Fund-driven national responses to HIV/AIDS in Liberia and Sierra Leone on the ABC approach to HIV prevention – Abstinence, Be faithful, and appropriate and consistent use of Condoms – may be of limited relevance given the pattern in which many young women are forced by socioeconomic circumstances and physical violence (especially rape) to have sex against their will. Such women are unlikely to seek voluntary HIV testing and counselling if they fear their partners would react violently if they proved to be HIV-positive, and nor are they likely to be able to be persuade their partners to use condoms. The fact that both countries' HIV programmes target high-risk groups such as sex workers, the military and ex-combatants in promoting condom use may also inadvertently stigmatise condoms and discourage their use by the general population.

Given the role of post-war trauma, especially among ex-combatants and wartime sexual assault survivors, in engendering further violence against women several years into post-conflict transitions, it is important for large-scale professional counselling and trauma management services to be instituted across Liberia and Sierra Leone. Since training professional psychiatrists and psychologists is a long-term project, innovative approaches involving lay counselling and behaviour modification therapy would also be necessary. Their sustainability will likely be enhanced if they are integrated from inception into existing social rehabilitation and reintegration programmes. This might require extended external technical assistance, given the desperate lack of human and institutional capacity in both countries after over a decade of armed conflict.[4] But such focused programming is likely to provide healing and enable more successful integration of ex-combatants and refugees. The potential benefits of healing and integration for stability and non-violence within intimate relationships may well be significant.

Given the concern over the sustainability of existing integrated responses to SGBV as the international development agencies that initiated them pull out of Liberia and Sierra Leone, it is important for central and provincial governments as well as international funding agencies to train the leaders and build the overall technical capacity of local women's organisations and human rights NGOs. These efforts should be geared towards their graduation from grassroots

---

4. Liberia, for example, by 2007 had only 51 physicians, 297 nurses and midwives and even fewer specialists in such areas as psychiatric care to cover a total population of nearly 3.5 million (GoL, 2008).

community mobilising to advocacy and service delivery organisations capable of serving hard-to-reach women at risk of SVAW and HIV. Expertise in establishing and managing legal clinics and protection arrangements for SVAW survivors would be especially valuable now that new rape laws have made it potentially easier to convict rapists.

Both countries also need massive behaviour-change communication campaigns to transform perceptions of gender roles and advance more equitable models of masculinity. In this regard, governments should partner with international reproductive health and education NGOs and donor agencies to review and expand the curricula of schools at all levels to include age-appropriate sexuality and gender education. To be effective, the content and delivery of such programmes should be shaped to introduce boys and girls to information and orientations favourable to the adoption of sexually healthy and violence-free gender relations.

Our analysis of the post-conflict experience of women and girls in Liberia and Sierra Leone also yields at least two lessons potentially applicable to new and future post-conflict transitions in other parts of Africa and elsewhere. First, it is critical that DDR programmes be designed to fully account for female ex-combatants and their rehabilitation and reintegration in order to break the cycle of repeat victimisation and oppression. For this to be successful, a longer term orientation to the community reintegration and rehabilitation aspects of DDR is needed to address the psychological effects of wartime involvement in combat. This would also help to counter the social ostracism often attached to women ex-combatants, especially those that return with children or physical disabilities.

Second, it is important to be aware of the significant upfront investment required to effectively address post-conflict SVAW on its own or in conjunction with HIV response. This is necessitated by the requirement for action across many sectors (health, education, justice systems, economic livelihoods enhancement) over a sustained period and progressively wider areas. Fairly effective small-scale programmes can be quickly mounted but would have to be rapidly scaled-up to the national level if the entrenched roots of SVAW in gender inequality are to be addressed and the vicious spiral of sexual violence experienced by women in wartime and for several years post-conflict is to be broken.

Overall, for women to be fully protected from sexual violence and HIV/AIDS in the transition to peace, our understanding of the gender dimensions of post-conflict transition dynamics needs to be further deepened. The new insights so generated must then be used to take action on several fronts that would require many more resources than are currently available for SVAW and gender inequality. Nonetheless, we know enough from recent experience in Liberia and Sierra Leone to prevent a repetition elsewhere of the sexual re-victimisation experienced by many women as a result of insufficient attention to the gender and human security aspects of post-conflict transition.

Summary and Conclusion

Despite the complexity of the intersections between armed conflict, post-conflict transitions and adult HIV prevalence at the aggregate level, the evidence is clear about the higher risks of HIV infection faced by individual women who are frequently exposed to sexual violence. Post-conflict transition in Liberia and Sierra Leone appears to have mainly produced a change in the forms and profile of the main perpetrators of SVAW, especially adolescents and pre-adolescents. Overall levels of chronic SVAW remain quite high.

It is therefore worrying that Liberia and Sierra Leone, like most other countries in Africa, attract far more external funding for HIV prevention and treatment programmes, which do not even modestly integrate responses to GBV and other critical gender equity issues. The required multisectoral responses to SVAW struggle to attract funding even after both countries have devised well thought-out national action plans for combating SVAW. This predicament calls into question the extent to which international assistance in post-conflict West Africa is informed by the evidence of the needs on the ground.

It is important to reiterate that overall levels of SVAW do not necessarily decline drastically even after many years of post-conflict transition. That in itself is a human rights, reproductive health and social welfare issue serious enough to raise questions about the validity of the presumed opportunities presented by post-conflict transitions to remake societies on the basis of human dignity and social justice.

References

Action Aid International (2007), *Show Us the Money: Is Violence Against Women on the HIV/AIDS Funding Agenda?* (Washington, DC: Action Aid).

Amnesty International (2008), *Liberia: A Flawed Process Discriminates against Women and Girls* (New York: Amnesty International).

— (2005), *Women in Post-Conflict Situations: A Fact Sheet* (New York: Amnesty International).

— (2001), *Sierra Leone: Rape and Other Forms of Sexual Violence against Girls and Women* (New York: AI).

Amowitz, L., C. Reis and K. Lyons *et al.* (2002), "Prevalence of War-Related Sexual Violence and Other Human Rights Abuses Among Internally Displaced Persons in Sierra Leone", *Journal of the American Medical Association*, 287(4):513-21.

Anema, A., M. Joffres, E. Mills and P. Spiegel (2008), "Widespread rape does not directly appear to increase the overall HIV prevalence in conflict-affected countries: so now what?", *Emerging Themes in Epidemiology*, 5(11).

Askew, I. (2006), *Addressing Sexual and Gender-Based Violence in a Development Context: Emerging Lessons and Issues in Africa* (New York: Population Council).

Barnes, K, P. Albrecht and M. Olson (2007), *Addressing Gender-Based Violence in Sierra Leone: Mapping Challenges, Responses and Future Entry Points* (Dublin: Irish Aid and International Alert).

Barnett, T. and G. Prins (2005), *HIV/AIDS and Security: Facts, Fiction and Evidence* (Geneva: UNAIDS).

Becker, J., C. Theodosis and R. Kulkarni (2008), "HIV/AIDS, conflict and security in Africa: rethinking relationships", *Journal of the International AIDS Society* 11(3).

Bekoe, D. and C. Paragon (2007), "Women's Role in Liberia's Reconstruction", *U.S. Institute for Peace Briefing Paper* May 2007 (Washington, DC: USIP).

Bertozzi, S., M. Laga *et al.* (2008), "Making HIV prevention programmes work", *Lancet* 372:831-844.

Bureau of Statistics and Institute for Resource Development (1988), *Liberia Demographic and Health Survey 1986: Final Report* (Monrovia: Bureau of Statistics and Columbia, MD: IRD).

Caldwell, J. and P. Caldwell (1993), "The nature and limits of the sub-Saharan Africa AIDS epidemic: evidence from geographic and other patterns", *Population and Development Review* 19(4):817-48.

Center for Health and Gender Equity (2002), *Gender-Based Violence and Reproductive Health and HIV/AIDS* (Washington, DC: CHANGE).

Chand, S. and R. Coffman (2008), "How Soon Can Donors Exit From Post-Conflict States?", *Working Paper No. 141* (Washington, DC: Center for Global Development).

Colletta, N., M. Kostner and I. Wiederhofer (1996), *The Transition from War to Peace in sub- Saharan Africa* (Washington, DC: World Bank).

Colombini, M. (2002), "Gender-based and Sexual Violence against women during Armed Conflict", *Journal of Health Management* 4(2):167-83).

Coulter, C., M. Persson and M. Utas (2008), *Young Female Fighters in African Wars: Conflict and Its Consequences* (Uppsala: Nordic Africa Institute).

Docking, T. (2001), "AIDS and Violent Conflict in Africa", *Special Report* – October 15 (Washington, DC: United States Institute of Peace).

Duvvury, N. (2005), "Gender Based Violence and HIV/AIDS: Links and Programs", Presentation at *Forum 9*, Mumbai, India, 12-16 September.

Elbe, S. (2003), *Strategic Implications of HIV/AIDS* [Adelphi Paper for the International Institute of Strategic Studies] (Oxford: Oxford University Press).

— (2002), "HIV/AIDS and the Changing Landscape of War in Africa", *International Security* 27(2):159-77.

Feldbaum, H., K. Lee and P. Patel (2006), "The National Security Implications of HIV/AIDS", *PLoS Medicine* 3(6):0774-0778.

Fithen, C. and P. Richards (2005), "Making War, Crafting Peace: Militia Solidarities and Demobilization in Sierra Leone", in P. Richards (ed.), *No Peace No War: Anthropology of Contemporary Armed Conflicts* (Athens: Ohio University Press and Oxford: James Currey): 117-40.

Fonck, K., L. Els *et al.* (2005), "Increased Risk of HIV in Women Experiencing Physical Partner Violence in Nairobi, Kenya", *AIDS and Behaviour* 9(3):335-9.

FRIDE (2007), *Justice for Women: Seeking Accountability for Sexual Crimes in Post-Conflict Situations* (Madrid: FRIDE).

Garrett, L. (2005), *HIV and National Security: Where are the Links?* (New York: Council on Foreign Relations).

Government of Liberia (2008), *A Poverty Reduction Strategy for Liberia* (Monrovia: GoL).

— (2006), *National Plan of Action for the Prevention and Management of Gender-Based Violence in Liberia* (Monrovia: GoL).

Government of Sierra Leone (2008), *Poverty Reduction Strategy for Sierra Leone: 2008-2010* (Freetown: GoSL).

— (2006), *Sierra Leone: Combined Initial, Second, Third, Fourth and Fifth Periodic Reports on CEDAW* (Freetown: GoSL).

— (2004), *Sierra Leone National HIV/AIDS Response Project* (Freetown: GoSL).

Henry, D. (2005), "The legacy of the tank: the violence of peace", *Anthropological Quarterly* 78(2):443-456.

Holst-Roness, F.T. (2007), "Conflict-driven violence against girls in Africa", *Forced Migration Review*, 27:26-9.

Ismail, O. (2008), "The Dynamics of Post-Conflict Reconstruction and Peace Building in West Africa: Between Change and Stability", *Discussion Paper* 41 (Uppsala: Nordic Africa Institute).

Jefferson, L.R. (2004), *In War as in Peace: Sexual Violence and Women's Status* Human Rights Watch World Report 2004 (New York: Human Rights Watch).

Johnson, K, J. Asher, S. Rosborough *et al.* (2008), "Association of Combatant Status and Sexual Violence With Mental and Mental Health Outcomes in Post-conflict Liberia", *Journal of the American Medical Association*, 300(6):676-90.

King, N. (2007), "Conflict as Integration: Youth Aspiration to Personhood in the Teleology of Sierra Leone's 'Senseless War'", *Current African Issues No. 36* (Uppsala: Nordic Africa Institute).

Klot, J. and P. DeLargy (2007), "Sexual violence and HIV/AIDS transmission", *Forced Migration Review* 27:23-4.

Koen, K. (2006), "Claiming space: Reconfiguring women's roles in post-conflict situations", *ISS Occasional Paper 121* (Pretoria: Institute for Security Studies).

Krug, E., L. Dahlberg, J. Mercy, A. Zwi and R. Lozano (2002), *World Report of Violence and Health* (Geneva: World Health Organization).

Liberia Institute of Statistics and Geo-Information Services and Macro International Inc. (2008), *Liberia Demographic and Health Survey 2007* (Monrovia and Calverton, MD: LISGIS and Macro International).

Macro International Inc. (2009), www.measuredhs.com (accessed 31 January 2009).

McInnes, C. (2009), "HIV, AIDS and Conflict in Africa: Why Isn't it (Even) Worse?", Paper presented at the Annual Conference of the International Studies Association, New York, February 2009.

Mazurana, D. and K. Carlson (2004), *From Combat to Community: Women and Girls of Sierra Leone* (Cambridge, MA: Hunt Alternatives Fund).

Michels, A. (2007), *Intersections of Sexual and Gender Based Violence and HIV/AIDS: Case Studies in the DRC, Liberia, Uganda and Colombia* (Rome: World Food Programme).

Ministry of Health and World Health Organization (2005), *Liberia Inter-Agency Health Evaluation: Final Report* (Monrovia: MoH and WHO).

Ministry of Planning and Economic Affairs and the United Nations Fund for Population Activities (2000), *Liberia Demographic and Health Survey 1999/2000: Analytical Report* (Monrovia: MPEA and UNFPA).

Nanjakululu, W.J. (2008), "Is AIDS an Artificial Epidemic, thriving in Conflict Situations?", Paper presented at the *XVII International AIDS Conference*, Mexico City, 4 August.

National AIDS Secretariat and United Nations Joint Programme on AIDS (2006), *HIV/AIDS Strategic Plan for Sierra Leone: 2006-2010* (Freetown: NAS and UNAIDS).

National AIDS and STI Control Program [Liberia] (2008), *Liberia Annual HIV and AIDS Review: 2007-08* (Monrovia: NASCP).

National Gender-Based Violence Committee (2008), *February 21-22 Retreat Report* (Freetown: N-GBV-C).

National Agency for the Control of AIDS [Nigeria] (2008), *2008 National HIV Sero-Prevalence Sentinel Survey among Antenatal Clinic Attendees: Preliminary Findings* (Abuja: NACA).

NEPAD Secretariat (2005), *African Post-Conflict Reconstruction Policy Framework* (Pretoria: NEPAD Secretariat).

Nilsson, D. (2003), "Liberia – The Eye of the Storm: A Review of the Literature on Internally Displaced, Refugees and Returnees", *Studies on Emergencies and Disaster Relief – Report No. 10* (Uppsala: Nordic Africa Institute).

Norberg, C. and C. Obi (2007), *Reconciling Winners and Losers in Post-Conflict Elections in West Africa: Political and Policy Imperatives* (Uppsala: Nordic Africa Institute).

Nzomo, M. (2002), *Gender, Governance and Conflicts in Africa* (Dakar: CODESRIA).

Obaid, T.A. (2007), "Introduction", *Forced Migration Review*, 27 (Special Issue on Sexual Violence: Weapon of War): 5-6.

Omanyondo, M.O. (2005), *Sexual Gender-Based Violence and Health Facility Needs Assessment in Liberia* (Monrovia: World Health Organization).

Oomman, N., M. Bernstein and S. Rosenzweig (2008), *Seizing the Opportunity on AIDS and Health Systems* (Washington, DC: Center for Global Development).

Physicians for Human Rights (2007), *Epidemic of Inequality: Women's Rights and HIV/AIDS in Botswana and Swaziland* (Cambridge, MA: PHR).

Piot, P. (2003), AIDS: *The Need for an Exceptional Response to an Unprecedented Crisis: A Presidential Fellows Lecture* (Washington, DC: World Bank and Geneva: UNAIDS).

Sawires, S.R. , S. Dworkin *et al.* (2007), "Male circumcision and HIV/AIDS: challenges and opportunities", *Lancet* 369: 708-13.

Schroven, A. (2006), *Women After War: Gender Mainstreaming and the Social Construction of Identity in Contemporary Sierra Leone* (Berlin: Lit Verlag).

Sesay, A. (2007), "Does One Size Fit All? The Sierra Leone Truth and Reconciliation Commission Revisited", *Discussion Paper 36* (Uppsala: Nordic Africa Institute).

Sejeebhoy, S. and S. Bold (2003), *Non-consensual Sexual Experiences of Young People: A Review from Developing Countries* (New Delhi: Population Council).

Spiegel, P.B. *et al.* (2007), "Prevalence of HIV infection in conflict-affected and displaced people in seven sub-Saharan African countries: a systematic review", *Lancet* 369(9580):2187-95.

Statistics Sierra Leone and Macro International Inc. (2008), *Sierra Leone Demographic and Health Survey 2008: Preliminary Report* (Freetown and Calverton, MD: SSL and Macro International).

United Nations Development Programme (2008), *The Human Development Report 2008* (New York: UNDP).

— (2007), *Liberia: National Human Development Report 2006* (Monrovia and New York: UNDP).

— (2002), *Gender Approaches in Conflict and Post-Conflict Situations* (New York: UNDP).

United Nations Fund for Population Activities (2006), *Programming to Address Violence Against Women* (New York: UNFPA).

United Nations Joint Programme on AIDS (2007), *2007 AIDS Epidemic Update* (Geneva: UNAIDS).

— (2006), *2006 AIDS Epidemic Update* (Geneva: UNAIDS).

— (2001), *HIV Prevention Needs and Successes: A Tale of Three Countries* (Geneva: UNAIDS).

United Nations Secretariat (2006), *Report of Panel Discussion: Addressing Sexual Violence in Liberia* (New York: UN Headquarters).

Ward, J (2002), *If Not Now, When? – Addressing Gender-based Violence in Refugee, Internally Displaced, and Post-conflict Settings: A Global Overview* (New York: Reproductive Health for Refugees Consortium).

Ward, J. and M. Marsh (2006), *Sexual Violence Against Women and Girls in War and Its Aftermath: Realities, Responses and Required Resources* (New York: UNFPA).

West African Network for Peace Building (2008), *A Situation Analysis of the Women Survivors of the 1989-2003 Conflict in Liberia* (Accra/Monrovia: WANEP).

Whiteside, A., A. De Waal, and T. Gebre-Tensae (2006), "AIDS, Security and the Military in Africa: A Sober Appraisal", *African Affairs* 105(419):201-18

Wilson, D. (2006), *HIV Epidemiology: A Review of Recent Trends and Lessons* (Washington, DC: World Bank).

Women's Commission for Refugee Women and Children (2004), *Liberia – Nothing Left to Lose: The Legacy of Armed Conflict and Landmines* (New York: WCRWC).

— (2002), *Precious Resources: Adolescents in the Reconstruction of Sierra Leone* (New York: WCRWC).

Zack-Williams, A.B., ed. (2008), *The Quest for Sustainable Development and Peace: The 2007 Sierra Leone Elections* (Uppsala: Nordic Africa Institute).

Bibliography

Abdullah, I. (2005) "'I am a Rebel". Youth Culture and Violence in Sierra Leone'. In A. Honwana and F. De Boeck (eds), *Makers and Breakers: Children and Youth in Postcolonial Africa*. Oxford/Trenton/Dakar: James Currey/Africa World Press/Codesria, pp. 172–87.

Abdullah, I. (1998) 'Bush Path to Destruction: The Origin and Character of the Revolutionary United Front/Sierra Leone', *Journal of Modern African Studies*, 36, 2(1998), pp. 203–35.

Abdullah, I. and P. Muana (1998) 'The Revolutionary United Front of Sierra Leone. A Revolt of the Lumpenproletariat'. In Clapham, C. (ed.), *African Guerillas*. Oxford/Kampala/Bloomington and Indianapolis: James Currey/Fountain Publishers/Indiana University Press, pp. 172–94.

Aboagye, F. (1999) *ECOMOG: A Sub-regional Experience in Conflict Resolution, Management and Peacekeeping in Liberia*, Accra.

Abraham, A. (2000) "The Quest for Peace in Sierra Leone." In *Engaging Sierra Leone, A Report by the Centre for Democracy and Development, London, CDD Strategy Planning Series 4*. London: CDD, pp. 12–36.

Addison, T. (2003) *Africa's Recovery from Conflict: Making Peace Work for the Poor*. Helsinki: UNU-WIDER.

Addison, T. (1998) 'Underdevelopment, Transition and Reconstruction in SSA', *UNU-WIDER Research for Action*, No. 45. Helsinki: UNU-WIDER.

Addison, T. and S.M. Murshed (t2001) 'From Conflict to Reconstruction: Reviving the Social Contract', *UNU-WIDER, Discussion Paper*, No. 2001/48. Helsinki: UNU-WIDER.

Adebajo, A. (2005) 'The Curse of Berlin: Africa's Security Dilemmas', *IPG* 4/2005.

Adebajo, A. (2004) 'Pax West Africana? Regional Security Mechanisms'. In Adebajo, A. And R. Ismail (eds), *West Africa's Security Challenges: Building Peace in A Troubled Region*. Boulder/London: Lynne Rienner for International Peace Academy, pp. 291–318.

Adebajo, A. (2002) 'Liberia: A Warlord's Peace'. In Stedman, J., D. Rothchild and E. Cousens (eds), *Ending Civil Wars: The Implementation of Peace Agreements*. Boulder/London: International Peace Academy and the Centre for International Security and Cooperation: Lynne Rienner, pp. 599–631.

Barnett, M. (2006) 'Building a Republican Peace: Stabilizing States after War', *International Security*, Vol. 30, No. 4, pp. 87–112.

BBC News/Africa, (13 December 2007), "Sierra Leone Orders Corruption Probe", available at http://news.bbc.co.uk/1/hi/world/africa/7141891.stm.

Bellamy, A. (2004) 'The Next Stage in Peace Operations Theory?' *International Peacekeeping*, Vol. 11, No. 1, pp. 17–38.

Bello, W. (2006) 'The Rise of the Relief-and-Reconstruction Complex', Columbia *Journal of International Affairs*, Vol. 59, No. 2, pp. 281–96.

Berdal, M. (1996) 'Disarmament and Demobilisation after Civil Wars', *Adelphi Paper* 303.

Berger, M. (2006) 'From Nation-Building to State-Building: The Geopolitics of Development, the Nation-state System and the Changing Global Order', *Third World Quarterly*, 27(1), pp. 5–25.

Berger, M. and H. Weber (2006) 'Beyond State-Building: Global Governance and the Crisis of the Nation-state System in the 21st Century', *Third World Quarterly,* 27(1), pp. 201–8.

Blagojevic, B. (2007) 'Peacebuilding in Ethnically Divided Societies', *Peace Review,* 19(4), pp. 555–62.

Boas, M. (2007) 'Marginalized Youth'. In Boas, M. and K. Dunn (eds), *African Guerrillas, Raging Against the Machine.* Boulder: Lynne Rienner, pp. 39–54.

Borer, T. (2006) 'Truth Telling as a Peacebuilding Activity: A Theoretical Overview'. In Borer (ed.), *Telling the Truths. Truth Telling and Peace Building in Post-Conflict Societies.* Notre Dame: University of Notre Dame, pp. 1–58.

Borer, T. et al. (2006) *Peacebuilding after Peace Accords: The Challenges of Violence, Truth, and Youth.* Notre Dame:University of Notre Dame Press.

Brzoska, M. (2006) 'Introduction: Criteria for Evaluating Post-Conflict Reconstruction and Security Sector Reform in Peace Support Operations', *International Peacekeeping,* 13(1), pp. 1–13.

Carbonnier, G. (1998) 'Conflict, Post-war Rebuilding and the Economy', *WIDER Occasional Paper* No. 2. Helsinki: WIDER.

Chandler, D. (2004) 'The Responsibility to Protect? Imposing the Liberal Peace', *International Peacekeeping,* Vol. 11, No. 1, pp. 59–81.

Chomsky, N. (2006) *Failed States: The Abuse of Power and Assault on Democracy.* London: Penguin.

Collier, P. (2004) 'Development and Security', Text of Public Lecture Delivered at 12th Bradford Development Lecture, Bradford Centre for International Development, Bradford University, UK, 11 November 2004.

Collier, P. and A. Hoeffler (2002) 'Aid, Policy and Peace: Reducing the Risks of Civil Conflict', *Defence and Peace Economics,* Vol. 13(6), pp. 435–50.

Collier, P. and A. Hoeffler (2001) *Greed and Grievance in Civil Wars.* US/UK: World Bank/CEPHR/CSAE. Available online at www.worldbank.org (search for author-s and title). Accessed 2 December 2003.

Cooper, N. (2005) 'Picking out the Pieces of the Liberal Peaces: Representations of Conflict Economies and the Implications for Policy', *Security Dialogue,* Vol. 36(4), pp. 463–78.

Coyne, C. (2006) 'Reconstructing Weak and Failed States', *The Journal of Social, Political and Economic Studies,* Vol. 31, No. 2 Summer 2006, pp. 143–62.

Curran, D. and T. Woodhouse (2007) 'Cosmopolitan Peacekeeping Peace building in Sierra Leone: What can Africa Contribute?' *International Affairs,* 83(6), pp. 1055–70.

Darby, J. (2006) 'The Post-Accord Context'. In Darby, J. (ed.), *Violence and Reconstruction.* Notre Dame: University of Notre Dame Press, pp. 1–10.

Dobbins, J. et al. (2007) *The Beginner's Guide to Nation-Building.* Santa Monica: RAND.

Dobbins, J. (2004) 'The UN's Role in Nation-building: From the Belgian Congo to Iraq', *Survival* Vol. 46, No. 4, Winter 2004–05, pp. 81–102.

Dobbins, J. (2003) 'America's Role in Nation-building: From Germany to Iraq', *Survival,* Vol. 45, No. 4, Winter 2003–04, pp. 87–110.

Dobbins, J. et al. (2003) *America's Role in Nation-building: From Germany to Iraq.* Santa Monica: RAND.

Dodge, T. (2006) 'Iraq: The Contradictions of Exogenous State-building in Historical Perspective', *Third World Quarterly,* 27(1), pp. 187–200.

Duffield, M. (2007) *Development, Security and Unending War: Governing the World of Peoples.* Cambridge: Polity Press.

Duffield, M. (2005) 'Social Reconstruction: The Reuniting of Aid and Politics', *Development,* 48(3), pp. 16–24.

Duffield, M. (2001) *Global Governance and the New Wars.* London/New York: Zed Books.

Dzelilovic, V. (2002) 'World Bank, NGOs and the Private Sector in Post-war Reconstruction', *International Peacekeeping,* 9(2), pp. 81–98.

ECOWAS (2001) *Protocol A/SP1/12/01 On Democracy and Good Governance.* Abuja: ECOWAS.

ECOWAS (1999) *Protocol Relating to the Mechanism for Conflict Prevention, Management, Resolution, Peacekeeping and Security.* Abuja: ECOWAS.

Edelstein, D. (2004) 'Occupational Hazards: Why Military Occupations Succeed or Fail', *International Security,* 29(1), pp. 49–91.

Etzioni, A. (2004) 'A Self-restrained Approach to Nation-building by Foreign Powers', International Affairs, 80(1), pp. 1–17.

Fanthorpe, R. (2005) 'On the Limits of Liberal Peace: Chiefs and Democratic Decentralization in Post-war Sierra Leone', *African Affairs,* 105/148, pp. 27–49.

Fetherston, A.B. (2000) 'Peacekeeping, Conflict Resolution and Peacebuilding: A Reconsideration of Theoretical Frameworks', *International Peacekeeping,* 7(1), pp. 190–218.

Forman, J. (2002) 'Achieving Socio-Economic Well-Being in Post-Conflict Settings', *Washington Quarterly,* 25, Autumn 2002, pp. 125–38.

The Foucault Effect. Hemel Hempstead: Harvester Wheatsheaf, pp. 87–104.

Foucault, M. (1991) 'Questions of Methods'. In Burchill, C., C. Gordon, P. Millar (eds), *The Foucault Effect.* Hemel Hempstead: Harvester Wheatsheaf, pp. 74–86.

Freeman, C. (2007) 'Introduction: Security, Governance and Statebuilding in Afghanistan', *International Peacekeeping,* 14(1), pp. 1–7.

Fukuyama, F. (2006) 'Nation-Building and the Failure of Institutional Memory'. In Fukuyama, F. (ed.), *Nation Building Beyond Afghanistan and Iraq.* Baltimore: Johns Hopkins University Press, pp. 1–18.

Fukuyama, F. (2005) *State-Building: Governance and World Order in the 21ˢᵗ Century.* London: Profile Books.

Galtung, J. (1964) 'A Structural Theory of Aggression', *Journal of Peace Research,* No. 2, pp. 95–119.

Gbla, O. (2006) 'Security Sector Reform under International Tutelage in Sierra Leone', *International Peacekeeping* 13(1), pp. 78–93.

Gennip, J. (2005) 'Post-conflict Reconstruction and Development', *Development* 48(3), pp. 57–62.

Goodhand, J. and M. Sedra (2007) 'Bribes or Bargains? Peace Conditionalities and "Post-Conflict" Reconstruction in Afghanistan', *International Peacekeeping,* Vol. 14, No. 1, pp. 41–61.

Gurr, T. (1970) *Why Men Rebel.* Princeton: Princeton University Press.

Guttal, S. (2005) 'The Politics of Post-war/Post-Conflict Reconstruction', *Development*, 48(3), pp. 73–81.

Hamre, J. and G. Sullivan (2002) 'Towards Post-Conflict Reconstruction', *Washington Quarterly*, 25(2002), pp. 85–96.

Hazen, J. (2007) 'Can Peacekeepers be Peacebuilders?' *International Peacekeeping* Vol. 14, No. 3, pp. 323–38.

Heathershaw, J. (2007) 'Peace building as Practice: Discourses from Post-conflict Tajikistan', *International Peacekeeping*, Vol. 14, No. 2, pp. 219–36.

Henry, P. (ed.), (1942) *Problems of Post War Reconstructio.* Washington: American Council on Public Affairs.

Howe, H. (2001) *Ambiguous Order. Military Forces in African States.* Boulder and London: Lynne Rienner.

ICG (2007) 'Sierra Leone: The Election Opportunity', *Africa Report*, No. 129, 12 July 2007.

ICG (2004) 'Liberia and Sierra Leone: Rebuilding Failed States', *Africa Report*, No. 87, 08 December 2004.

ICG (2003) 'Sierra Leone: The State of Security and Governance', *Africa Report*, No. 67, 02 September 2003.

ICG (2002) 'Sierra Leone after Elections: Politics as Usual?' *Africa Report*, No. 49, 15 July 2002.

IRIN News (14 May 2007) "GUINEA: Soldiers Continue Looting after President Concedes to Demands", http://www.irinnews.org/Report.aspx?ReportId=72138.

Ismail, O. (2003) *The Day After: Child Soldiers in Post-war Sierra Leone.* Report submitted to the SSRC, New York, African Youth in the Era of Globalization Fellowship Programme.

Jonah, J. (2004) The United Nations. in Adebajo, A. and R. Ismail (eds), *West Africa's Security Challenges. Building Peace in a Troubled Region.* Boulder and London: Lynne Rienner, pp. 319–348.

Jones, S. et al. (2005) *Establishing Law and Order after Conflict.* Santa Monica: RAND.

Joseph, R. (1999) 'The Reconfiguration of Power in Late Twentieth-Century Africa'. In Joseph, R. (ed.), *State, Conflict and Democracy in Africa.* Boulder/London: Lynne Rienner, pp. 57–82.

Kaldor, M. (2001) *New and Old Wars: Organized Violence in a Global Era.* Stanford: Stanford University Press.

Kang, S. and J. Meernik (2004) 'Determinants of Post-Conflict Economic Assistance', *Journal of Peace Research*, Vol. 41, No. 2, pp. 149–66.

Keane, J. (2004) *Violence and Democracy.* Cambridge: Cambridge University Press.

Keen, D. (2008) *Complex Emergencies.* London: Polity Press.

Keen, D. (2003) 'Greedy Elites, Dwindling Resources, Alienated Youths: The Anatomy of Protracted Violence in Sierra Leone', *International Politics and Society (IPG)*, 2/2003.

Keen, D. (2000) 'War and Peace: What's the Difference?' *International Peacekeeping*, 7(4), pp. 1–22.

Klingebiel, S. (2005) 'Africa's New Peace and Security Architecture', *African Security Review*, 14(2), pp. 35–44.

Krause, K. and O. Jutersonke (2005) 'Peace, Security and Development in Post-Conflict Environments', *Security Dialogue,* Vol. 36, No.4, pp. 447–62.

Last, D. (2000) in Ramsbotham, O. et al., *The Bergerhof Handbook for Conflict Transformation.* Germany: Bergerhof Research Centre for Constructive Conflict Management.

Lederach, J.P. (2003) *The Little Book of Conflict Transformation.* Intercourse: Good Books.

Malone, D. and K. Wermester (2000) 'Boom and Bust? The Changing Nature of UN Peacekeeping', *International Peacekeeping,* 7(4), pp. 37–54.

Mani, R. (2005) 'Balancing Peace with Justice in the Aftermath of Violent Conflict', *Development* 48(3), pp. 25–34.

Mani, R. (2005) 'Rebuilding an Inclusive Political Community after War', *Security Dialogue,* Vol. 36(4), pp. 511–26.

McEvoy-Levy, S. (2006) 'Introduction: Youth and the Post-Accord Environment'. In McEvoy-Levy, S. (ed.), *Troublemakers or Peacemakers? Youth and Post-Accord Peace Building.* Notre Dame: University of Notre Dame, pp. 1–26.

McMullin, J. (2004) 'Reintegration of Combatants: Were the Right Lessons Learned in Mozambique?' *International Peacekeeping,* Vol. 11, No. 4, pp. 625–43.

Miall, H. et al. (1999) *Contemporary Conflict Resolution.* London: Polity Press.

Montgomery, J. and D. Rondinelli (2004) 'A Path to Reconstruction: Proverbs of Nation-building', *Harvard International Review,* Summer 2004, pp. 26–9.

Moran, M. (2006) *Liberia: The Violence of Democracy.* Philadelphia: University of Pennsylvania Press.

National Recovery Strategy (NRS) Sierra Leone 2002–2003 (n.d).

Natsios, A. (2005) 'The Nine Principles of Reconstruction and Development', *Parameters,* Autumn 2005, pp. 4–20.

Nitzschke, H. and K. Studdard (2005) 'The Legacies of War Economies: Challenges and Options for Peacemaking and Peace building', *International Peacekeeping,* Vol. 12, No. 2, pp. 222–39.

Olonisakin, F. (2008) *Peacekeeping in Sierra Leone: The Story of UNAMSIL.* Boulder/London: Lynne Rienner for International Peace Academy.

Olonisakin, F. (2000) 'Reinventing Peacekeeping in Africa. Conceptual and Legal Issues in ECOMOG Operations'. Hague/London/Boston: Kluwer Law International.

Paris, R. (2004) *At War's End: Building Peace after Civil Conflict.* New York: Cambridge University Press.

Pearce, J. (2005) 'The International Community and Peacebuilding', *Development* 48(3), pp. 41–9.

Peters, K. and P. Richards (1998) 'Why We Fight: Voices of Youth Combatants in Sierra Leone', *Africa,* Vol. 68, No. 2, pp. 183–210.

Plattner, M. (2005) 'Building Democracy after Conflict: Introduction', *Journal of Democracy,* Vol. 16, No. 1, pp. 5–8.

Poku, N. et al. (2007) 'Human Security and Development in Africa', *International Affairs* 83(6), pp. 1155–70.

Pouligny, B. (2005) 'Civil Society and Post-Conflict Peacebuilding: Ambiguities of International Programmes Aimed at Building "New" Societies', *Security Dialogue* Vol. 36(4), pp. 495–510.

Pugh, M. (2004) 'Peacekeeping and Critical Theory', *International Peacekeeping*, Vol. 11, No. 1, pp. 39–58.

Ramsbotham, O. (2000) 'Reflections on UN Post-Settlement Peacebuilding', *International Peacekeeping*, 7(1), pp. 169–89.

Reilly, B. (2002) 'Post-Conflict Elections: Constraints and Dangers', *International Peacekeeping*, 9(2), pp. 118–39.

Reno, W. (2003) 'Political Networks in a Failing State: The Roots and Future of Violent Conflict in Sierra Leone', *International Politics and Society (IPG)*, 2/2003.

Reno, W. (1998) *Warlord Politics and African States*. Boulder: Lynne Rienner.

Republic of Liberia (n.d.) *Interim Poverty Reduction Strategy. Breaking with the Past: From Conflict to Development*. Liberia.

Richards, P. (1995) 'Rebellion in Liberia and Sierra Leone: A Crisis of Youth?' In Furley, O. (ed.), *Conflict in Africa*. London/New York: Tauris, pp. 134–70.

Richards, P. (1996) *Fighting for the Rain Forest: War Youth and Resources in Sierra Leone*. London: International African Institute and James Currey.

Richmond, O. (2004) 'UN Peace Operations and the Dilemmas of the Peacebuilding Consensus', *International Peacekeeping* 11(1), pp. 83–101.

Ross, D. (2004) *Violent Democracy*, Cambridge: Cambridge University Press.

Rubinstein, R. (2005) 'Intervention and Culture: An Anthropological Approach to Peace Operations', *Security Dialogue*, Vol. 36, No. 4, pp. 527–44.

Runciman, W. (1966) *Relative Deprivation and Social Justice*. London: Routledge and Kegan Paul.

Ryan, S. (2000) 'United Nations Peacekeeping: A Matter of Principles?' *International Peacekeeping*, 7(1), pp. 27–47.

Sawyer, A. (2005) *Beyond Plunder: Towards Democratic Governance in Liberia*. Boulder/London: Lynne Rienner.

Schnabel, A. (2002) 'Post-Conflict Peacebuilding and Second-Generation Preventive Action', *International Peacekeeping*, 9(2), pp. 7–30.

Schwarz, R. (2005) 'Post-Conflict Peacebuilding: The Challenges of Security, Welfare and Representation', *Security Dialogue*, Vol. 36, No. 4, pp. 429–46.

Simonsen, S. (2004) 'Nation-building as Peacebuilding: Racing to Define the Kosovar', *International Peacekeeping*, 11(2), pp. 289–311.

SIPRI (2002) *SIPRI Year Book 2002: Armaments, Disarmament and International Security*. Oxford: Oxford University Press.

Sorensen, B. (1998) Women and Post-Conflict Reconstruction, *WIDER Occasional Paper No. 3*. Geneva: WIDER.

Sriram, C. (2000) 'Truth Commissions and the Quest for Justice: Stability and Accountability after Internal Strife', *International Peacekeeping*, 7(4), pp. 91–106.

Stedman, J. (2002) 'Introduction'. In Stedman, J., D. Rothchild and E. Cousens (eds), *Ending Civil Wars: The Implementation of Peace Agreements*. Boulder/London: International Peace Academy and the Centre for International Security and Cooperation: Lynne Rienner, pp. 1–42.

Stedman, J., D. Rothchild and E. Cousens (eds), (2002) *Ending Civil Wars: The Implementation of Peace Agreements*. Boulder/London: International Peace Academy and the Centre for International Security and Cooperation: Lynne Rienner.

The Courier (2003) 'Post-conflict Rehabilitation', No. 198, May–June 2003.

Tull, D. and A. Mehler (2005) 'The Hidden Costs of Power-Sharing: Reproducing Insurgent Violence in Africa', *African Affairs*, 104/416, pp. 375–98.

Ugo, P. 1947. *Introduction to Post-war Reconstruction Programme.* Rome: International Institute of Agriculture.

United Nations (20 Dec 2005) UN Security Council Resolution 1645, S/RES/1645 (2005), http://daccessdds.un.org/doc/UNDOC/GEN/N05/654/17/PDF/N0565417. pdf?OpenElement.

United Nations (1997) Supplement to An Agenda for Peace, A/RES/51/242, 15 September 1997, http://www.un.org/documents/ga/res/51/a51r242.htm.

United Nations (1995) A Supplement to the Agenda for Peace, A/50/60-S/1995/1, 03 January 1995, http://www.un.org/Docs/SG/agsupp.html.

United Nations (1992) An Agenda for Peace, A/47/277-S/24111, 17 June 1992, http://www.un.org/Docs/SG/agpeace.html.

Wentges, J. (1998) 'Force, Function and Phase: Three Dimensions of UN Peacekeeping', *International Peacekeeping*, Vol. 5, No. 3, pp. 58–77.

Whiteman, K. and D. Yates (2004) 'France, Britain, and the United States'. In Adebajo, A. and Ismail, R. (eds), *West Africa's Security Challenges. Building Peace in a Troubled Region.* Boulder and London: Lynne Rienner, pp. 349–82.

Williams, A. (2005) 'Reconstruction' before the Marshall Plan', *Review of International Studies,* 31, pp. 541–58.

Williams, G. (2005) *Engineering Peace: The Military Role in Post-conflict Reconstruction.* Washington: USIP.

Williams, P. (2004) 'Peace Operations and the International Financial Institutions: Insights from Rwanda and Sierra Leone', *International Peacekeeping,* 11(1), pp. 103–23.

Williams, R. (2000) 'Africa and the Challenges of Security Sector Reform'. In Cilliers, J. and A. Hilding-Norberg (eds), *Building Stability in Africa: Challenges for the new millennium.* ISS Monograph 46. Pretoria: Institute for Security Studies.

Woodhouse, T. and O. Ramsbotham (2005) 'Cosmopolitan Peacekeeping and the Globalization of Security', *International Peacekeeping*, Vol. 12, No. 2, pp. 139–56.

World Bank (August 1998) *Conflict Prevention and Post-Conflict Reconstruction: Perspectives and Prospects.* Paris: World Bank Post-Conflict Unit.

Yannis, A. (2003) 'State Collapse and its Implications for Peace Building and Reconstruction'. In Milliken, J. (ed.), *State Failure, Collapse and Reconstruction.* Oxford: Blackwell, pp. 63–82.

Young, C. (2004) 'The End of the Post-Colonial State in Africa? Reflections on Changing African Political Dynamics', *African Affairs*, 103, pp. 23–49.

Youngs, R. (2004) 'Democratic Institution-Building and Conflict Resolution: Emerging EU Approaches', *International Peacekeeping*, Vol. 11, No. 3, pp. 536–43.

Zanotti, L. (2006) 'Taming Chaos: A Foucauldian View of UN Peacekeeping, Democracy and Normalization', *International Peacekeeping,* 13(2), pp. 150–67.

Zartman, I. (1995) 'Posing the Problem of State Collapse'. In Zartman. I. (ed.), *Collapsed States: The Disintegration and Restoration of Legitimate Authority.* Boulder: Lynne Rienner, pp. 1–14.

DISCUSSION PAPERS PUBLISHED BY THE INSTITUTE

Recent issues in the series are available electronically for download free of charge
www.nai.uu.se

1. Kenneth Hermele and Bertil Odén, *Sanctions and Dilemmas. Some Implications of Economic Sanctions against South Africa.* 1988. 43 pp. ISBN 91-7106-286-6

2. Elling Njål Tjönneland, *Pax Pretoriana. The Fall of Apartheid and the Politics of Regional Destabilisation.* 1989. 31 pp. ISBN 91-7106-292-0

3. Hans Gustafsson, Bertil Odén and Andreas Tegen, *South African Minerals. An Analysis of Western Dependence.* 1990. 47 pp. ISBN 91-7106-307-2

4. Bertil Egerö, *South African Bantustans. From Dumping Grounds to Battlefronts.* 1991. 46 pp. ISBN 91-7106-315-3

5. Carlos Lopes, *Enough is Enough! For an Alternative Diagnosis of the African Crisis.* 1994. 38 pp. ISBN 91-7106-347-1

6. Annika Dahlberg, *Contesting Views and Changing Paradigms.* 1994. 59 pp. ISBN 91-7106-357-9

7. Bertil Odén, *Southern African Futures. Critical Factors for Regional Development in Southern Africa.* 1996. 35 pp. ISBN 91-7106-392-7

8. Colin Leys and Mahmood Mamdani, *Crisis and Reconstruction – African Perspectives.* 1997. 26 pp. ISBN 91-7106-417-6

9. Gudrun Dahl, *Responsibility and Partnership in Swedish Aid Discourse.* 2001. 30 pp. ISBN 91-7106-473-7

10. Henning Melber and Christopher Saunders, *Transition in Southern Africa – Comparative Aspects.* 2001. 28 pp. ISBN 91-7106-480-X

11. *Regionalism and Regional Integration in Africa.* 2001. 74 pp. ISBN 91-7106-484-2

12. Souleymane Bachir Diagne, et al., *Identity and Beyond: Rethinking Africanity.* 2001. 33 pp. ISBN 91-7106-487-7

13. Georges Nzongola-Ntalaja, et al., *Africa in the New Millennium.* Edited by Raymond Suttner. 2001. 53 pp. ISBN 91-7106-488-5

14. *Zimbabwe's Presidential Elections 2002.* Edited by Henning Melber. 2002. 88 pp. ISBN 91-7106-490-7

15. Birgit Brock-Utne, *Language, Education and Democracy in Africa.* 2002. 47 pp. ISBN 91-7106-491-5

16. Henning Melber et al., *The New Partnership for Africa's Development (NEPAD).* 2002. 36 pp. ISBN 91-7106-492-3

17. Juma Okuku, *Ethnicity, State Power and the Democratisation Process in Uganda.* 2002. 42 pp. ISBN 91-7106-493-1

18. Yul Derek Davids, et al., *Measuring Democracy and Human Rights in Southern Africa.* Compiled by Henning Melber. 2002. 50 pp. ISBN 91-7106-497-4

19. Michael Neocosmos, Raymond Suttner and Ian Taylor, *Political Cultures in Democratic South Africa.* Compiled by Henning Melber. 2002. 52 pp. ISBN 91-7106-498-2

20. Martin Legassick, *Armed Struggle and Democracy. The Case of South Africa.* 2002. 53 pp. ISBN 91-7106-504-0

21. Reinhart Kössler, Henning Melber and Per Strand, *Development from Below. A Namibian Case Study.* 2003. 32 pp. ISBN 91-7106-507-5

22. Fred Hendricks, *Fault-Lines in South African Democracy. Continuing Crises of Inequality and Injustice.* 2003. 32 pp. ISBN 91-7106-508-3

23. Kenneth Good, *Bushmen and Diamonds. (Un)Civil Society in Botswana.* 2003. 39 pp. ISBN 91-7106-520-2

24. Robert Kappel, Andreas Mehler, Henning Melber and Anders Danielson, *Structural Stability in an African Context.* 2003. 55 pp. ISBN 91-7106-521-0

25. Patrick Bond, *South Africa and Global Apartheid. Continental and International Policies and Politics.* 2004. 45 pp. ISBN 91-7106-523-7

26. Bonnie Campbell (ed.), *Regulating Mining in Africa. For whose benefit?* 2004. 89 pp. ISBN 91-7106-527-X

27. Suzanne Dansereau and Mario Zamponi, *Zimbabwe – The Political Economy of Decline.* Compiled by Henning Melber. 2005. 43 pp. ISBN 91-7106-541-5

28. Lars Buur and Helene Maria Kyed, *State Recognition of Traditional Authority in Mozambique. The Nexus of Community Representation and State Assistance.* 2005. 30 pp. ISBN 91-7106-547-4

29. Hans Eriksson and Björn Hagströmer, *Chad – Towards Democratisation or Petro-Dictatorship?* 2005. 82 pp. ISBN 91-7106-549-0

30. Mai Palmberg and Ranka Primorac (eds), *Skinning the Skunk – Facing Zimbabwean Futures.* 2005. 40 pp. ISBN 91-7106-552-0

31. Michael Brüntrup, Henning Melber and Ian Taylor, *Africa, Regional Cooperation and the World Market – Socio-Economic Strategies in Times of Global Trade Regimes.* Compiled by Henning Melber. 2006. 70 pp. ISBN 91-7106-559-8

32. Fibian Kavulani Lukalo, *Extended Handshake or Wrestling Match? – Youth and Urban Culture Celebrating Politics in Kenya.* 2006. 58 pp. ISBN 91-7106-567-9

33. Tekeste Negash, *Education in Ethiopia: From Crisis to the Brink of Collapse.* 2006. 55 pp. ISBN 91-7106-576-8

34. Fredrik Söderbaum and Ian Taylor (eds), *Micro-Regionalism in West Africa. Evidence from Two Case Studies.* 2006. 32 pp. ISBN 91-7106-584-9

35. Henning Melber (ed.), *On Africa – Scholars and African Studies.* 2006. 68 pp. ISBN 978-91-7106-585-8

36. Amadu Sesay, *Does One Size Fit All? The Sierra Leone Truth and Reconciliation Commission Revisited.* 2007. 56 pp. ISBN 978-91-7106-586-5

37. Karolina Hulterström, Amin Y. Kamete and Henning Melber, *Political Opposition in African Countries – The Case of Kenya, Namibia, Zambia and Zimbabwe.* 2007. 86 pp. ISBN 978-7106-587-2

38. Henning Melber (ed.), *Governance and State Delivery in Southern Africa. Examples from Botswana, Namibia and Zimbabwe.* 2007. 65 pp. ISBN 978-91-7106-587-2

39. Cyril Obi (ed.), *Perspectives on Côte d'Ivoire: Between Political Breakdown and Post-Conflict Peace.* 2007. 66 pp. ISBN 978-91-7106-606-6

40. Anna Chitando, *Imagining a Peaceful Society. A Vision of Children's Literature in a Post-Conflict Zimbabwe.* 2008. 26 pp. ISBN 978-91-7106-623-7

41. Olawale Ismail, *The Dynamics of Post-Conflict Reconstruction and Peace Building in West Africa. Between Change and Stability.* 2009. 52 pp. ISBN 978-91-7106-637-4

42. Ron Sandrey and Hannah Edinger, *Examining the South Africa–China Agricultural Trading Relationship.* 2009. 58 pp. ISBN 978-91-7106-643-5

43. Xuan Gao, *The Proliferation of Anti-Dumping and Poor Governance in Emerging Economies.* 2009. 41 pp. ISBN 978-91-7106-644-2

44. Lawal Mohammed Marafa, *Africa's Business and Development Relationship with China. Seeking Moral and Capital Values of the Last Economic Frontier.* 2009. 21 pp. ISBN 978-91-7106-645-9

45. Mwangi wa Githinji, *Is That a Dragon or an Elephant on Your Ladder? The Potential Impact of China and India on Export Led Growth in African Countries.* 2009. 40 pp. ISBN 978-91-7106-646-6

46. Jo-Ansie van Wyk, *Cadres, Capitalists, Elites and Coalitions. The ANC, Business and Development in South Africa.* 2009. 61 pp. ISBN 978-91-7106-656-5

47. Elias Courson, *Movement for the Emancipation of the Niger Delta (MEND). Political Marginalization, Repression and Petro-Insurgency in the Niger Delta.* 2009. 30 pp. ISBN 978-91-7106-657-2

48. Babatunde A. Ahonsi, *Gender Violence and HIV/AIDS in Post-Conflict West Africa.* 2010, 38 pp. ISBN 978-91-7106- 665-7

www.ingramcontent.com/pod-product-compliance
Lightning Source LLC
Chambersburg PA
CBHW080209300326
41934CB00039B/3436